CARUSI

The Shame of Sicily

Louis Romano

Louis Romano   Carusi: The Shame of Sicily

ISBN: 978-1-944906-21-4

Printed in the U.S.A. First Edition, 2018 Vecchia Publishing

1

Other Books by Louis Romano

Detective Vic Gonnella Series

INTERCESSION

YOU THINK I'M DEAD

JUSTIFIED

Gino Ranno Series

FISH FARM

BESA

GAME OF PAWNS

EXCLUSION: THE FIGHT FOR CHINATOWN

Zip Code Series

ZIP CODE

Short Story & Poetry Series

Anxiety's Nest

Anxiety's Cure

ACKNOWLEDGMENTS

This is my twelfth book and the one which has the most people to recognize.

My dear friend Ken Festa took a trip with me to Sicily for much of the research that was needed to get the real feel of what went on in the sulfur mines. His advice and passion for this work was fabulous.

In Lercara Friddi, Sicily, my ancestral home, I am very grateful to my cousins Antonella Miceli and her husband Filippo Rubaudo who were the best hosts and advisors I could possibly imagine. Without Filippo, there would be no book. He helped me gather so much information before, during, and after my trip to Sicily. I could never have written this without his help.

My translator and distant cousin, Josephine "Jo" Greco was my right hand in Sicily. She was there every step of the way and assisted with research well after I returned home.

Pippo Furnari was an enormous help with my research. His brilliant mind and recall of the history of the sulfur mines was a tremendous help.

The current Mayor of Lercara Friddi, Giuseppe Ferrara welcomed me "home" with a wonderful day at his office. I wish him well for his reelection.

My sincere thanks to three carusi I interviewed, Nicolo Di Salvo, Tommaso Licata, and Antonino Lucania, whose stories about their labor in the mines were heart wrenching. These men told their stories of working in the hellish environment of the sulfur mines of Lercara Friddi.

A wonderful young man and guide, Giuseppe Bosco spent hours with us at a mine near Agrigento. He and I have become great Facebook pen pals.

My pre readers all gave their input and advice to this book.

Ellen Festa, read the manuscript and did initial editing giving critical advice and correction, which helped enormously.

The entire voyage of this book is because of Kathleen Collins, who read a short story I'd written on the carusi. Her insistence that a short story was simply not enough was the reason I wrote this entire book. I am forever grateful for Kathleen's guidance and patience with me during the research and writing of this book, as well as the final editing.

My fourteen-year-old Jack Russell, Rocco was at my feet throughout most of the writing as he has been for every publication. I hope he has at least one or two more books left in him.

My entire family was super supportive throughout the entire process.

Lastly, I want to thank my great-grandparents, Pietro Miceli and Dorotea Salerno, who both passed away before I was born, for taking our family on the difficult and emotional journey to America.

My Grandfather, Gaspare Miceli

My Great-Grandmother, Dorotea Salerno Miceli

When Louis involved me in his project to write a book about the Carusi of the sulphur mines in Lercara Friddi I was immediately infected by his enthusiasm.

Therefore, I immersed myself into the research for the historical and social events of the Lercarese community between the late nineteenth and early twentieth centuries. I am not from Lercara but I love this land and its people so much as if I were, so I carried out this project with interest and dedication.

While the research proceeded with good results, I realized that the more I immersed Louis with news and events, the more his thirst for knowledge grew.

I realize now that even before writing his book Louis' great need was the research and knowledge of his origins, man's roots and his belonging to a family. Louis, do you remember the Via Cimò?

Filippo Ribaudo

Meeting Louis was a pleasure and an honor for me. This experience has made me feel part of something special: the birth of a book about Lercara and how difficult life was in my hometown at the end of the 1800s.

While translating Louis' questions visiting the abandoned mines and meeting the old miners I could see the expression of his eyes change from enthusiasm to curiosity, from astonishment to sadness and bitterness.

I am sure that each and every emotion that he experienced helped him to write his book with passion and dedication giving voice to the Carusi.

Josephine Greco

When my friend Filippo Ribaudo asked me if I was willing to meet his cousin, "an American" whose great grandparents were born in Lercara, to exchange some information about the sulphur mines I thought of a nostalgic person who would ask me the same questions about the Carusi and when the mines were closed.

I was tremendously wrong. Louis had an incredible baggage of knowledge about the mines and the miners.

His questions were determined, precise and he was eager to know details about the miners' everyday lives but also to contextualize the historical period.

We talked about the miners' lives, the working conditions and the organization in the mines, but also about the workers' struggles and the "Fasci Siciliani" Movement in Lercara and the Christmas Day Massacre in 1893.

We all owe much to Louis for his dedication, his research and his energy to a world which no longer exists.

His novel will surely make the Sulphur civilization relive, which for two centuries marked the Sicilian society and in particular that of Lercara.

Pippo Furnari

"I am not prepared just now to say to what extent I believe in a physical hell in the next world, but a sulphur mine in Sicily is about the nearest thing to hell that I expect to see in this life."

-Booker Taliaferro Washington

A Note From the Author

In the mid-to-late nineteenth century, the island of Sicily produced ninety percent of a mineral that did everything from dying fabrics for a booming global textile industry, to making pesticides, to making gunpowder for mankind's never-ending conflicts.

Just north of Agrigento, Sicily is the small town of Favara, the abandoned Ciavolotta sulfur mines dot the landscape like monuments to the brutality that came along with the essential mineral.

As I was researching the lives of the carusi, the five to sixteen-year old boys who were forced by abject poverty into indentured servitude in the sulfur mines, I was led to a chapel dedicated to St. Barbara the patron Saint of miners.

After I left the cave-like chapel, replete with a large plaster statue of the saint, her garments painted in light violet and white, with a gold sash and crown, the base of the statue surrounded by fresh flowers and votive candles, my guide noticed there was a small brown spider on my shirt. He gently brushed the tiny creature from my shirt and we continued surveying the exterior grounds of the mines. In my mind's eye, I could see the lumbering piccionere entering the mines with their heavy pick axes followed by the barefoot and barely clothed carusi, descending into the hell-like world below.

An hour later, after gathering samples, dropping stones into a vent that seemed to have no bottom and hearing about the lives of the mine owners, managers, piccionere and carusi, the guide brought up the spider.

"It is considered good fortune for you that the spider came onto your shirt," he said in Sicilian dialect.

"Good luck is always welcome," I replied.

"You must go back into the chapel and write down on a paper to Santa Barbara what you want. Money will then come to you."

A second guide, understanding the superstition without comment, unbolted the heavy, black iron and glass door for me to re-enter. To the right of the statue, there was a clear, glass vase that missed my attention on the first visit. Inside the case were folded papers that called upon the saint's intercession for favors that would be ostensibly fulfilled by someone in the Holy Trinity.

The second guide provided the paper and pencil and turned his back so I could have privacy with St. Barbara and my thoughts and prayers. I wrote the following:

"Cara Santa Barbara…Please guide me to write a book worthy of the memory of the carusi."

CHAPTER 1

I remember everything.

Still today, in the year 1975, as a very old man of ninety-one, I remember everything.

I remember the night before my Papà died. He was such a good Papà He worked all the time and never complained, never raised his voice or spanked us like other fathers did. He had a gentle manner about him and he loved to hear us tell stories about our day and what we were learning about plants, animals, and people. I would look at the sky at night with Papà and try to make out figures from the stars and call them by the special names which we gave them. Papà promised to teach me the friscalettu, his handmade flute, for Christmas, so I could play for our friends and relatives.

All I wanted to be happy in my life, was to be like my Papà.

It was a Friday night when I last held Papà and kissed his cheek before going to sleep. Funny, but I remember Papà held me a bit longer than usual that night. Then, a strange thing happened. Just as me and my brothers and sister fell asleep, we awoke to him sitting on the edge of our mattress, singing our favorite song and playing his friscalettu.

Sciuri, sciuri, sciuri di tutu l'annu
l'amuri ca mi dasti ti lu tornu.
Sciuri, sciuri, sciuri di tuttu l'annu
l'amuri ca mi dasti ti lu tornu.
La-la-laralla, la-la-la-la-la-la.

We jumped out of bed, clapping and singing along with Papà. Mama wanted us to get back to sleep, or maybe she wanted to be alone with Papà for a few minutes, but Papà kept laughing and singing for the longest time.

I fell asleep and dreamt of singing and dancing with Papà as he walked to his work.

Papà had gone to work before the sun came up the next morning, as he always did. We never saw Papà again.

I was four years old in the year 1888 when Papà didn't return home from the sulfur mine in the town where I was born, Lercara Friddi, Sicily. There was an explosion in the mine and forty-three picconiere, the men who chipped away at the walls of the mine, and one hundred and ten carusi, the young boys who carried the sulfur ore to the surface, all died.

Twenty carusi lived to work again. They were the lucky ones who were outside the mine bringing ore to the calcaroni, a large furnace where the ore was processed. Or maybe they were not so lucky after all.

No one was going to dig down into that mine to see if any of the men or boys survived the explosion and the cave in. This had happened before at the mines. The carusi and the picconiere who perished were left where they died. All these years later, I still imagine them all gasping for their last breath of air before they choked to death.

I can still hear the wailing and screaming that came from my Mama and the other women who lost their husbands, sons, and brothers that day.

Everyone in town started running toward the mine at the foot of the Colle Madore, the highest mountain in Lercara. It's strange what I often think of now. My Papà promised to take me up on the Colle Madore one day. He said the mountain was so high that on a clear day we could see Mount Etna on the other side of Sicily. I never did get up there to see Etna.

I recall running along with the townspeople, hearing the shrill sound of the mine's whistle, alerting everyone there was trouble. Everything seemed to move very quickly until we got to the mine, out of breath and out of our minds with worry.

Monsignor Giacomo Paci, the archpriest from the church in the main square of town, Santa Maria Della Neve, Our Lady of the Snow, zoomed by us in a horse drawn carriage, along with two carabinieri and Signore Sartorio, the mayor of Lercara Friddi. The grim-faced mayor held onto his hat. The priest's black cassock flapped in the wind like a giant, flying bird. The carabinieri fought hard to control the horses.

When we arrived at the mine, the crowd was enormous. Monsignor Paci was on his knees, on the dusty, barren ground, rosary in hand, his mouth moving quickly in prayer. I always thought he was acting for the crowd and not really concerned for the surfarari, the miners.

The dead were not even permitted a funeral at the church because their deaths were considered violent. No matter, the bodies were never recovered.

Nothing could grow anywhere near the mine after the combustion of sulfur from the calcaroni. The entire area resembled a brown and gray desert with nothing green on the ground.

Signore Sartorio was deep in conversation with Signore Giuseppe Modica, the boss of the mine, a brutal man who everyone tipped their hats to. Signore Modica was a squat man with a dark complexion, big stomach and piercing blue eyes. Papà always said Signore Modica was a man that required respect, but when I think back now, it was more fear that the workers felt. Fear and hatred.

It was a hot, July day, and the blazing sun was not at all sympathetic to the tragedy.

I stood next to my Mama as she wrung her hands and prayed to Santa Barbara, the patron saint of miners and Our Lady of Constantinople, the patron saint of our town, hoping against hope Papà and the others would find their way to the surface. Mama's long, brown skirt was tattered, but clean, flowing down to her bare feet. Her white blouse clung to her body, her beautiful, chestnut-brown hair matted with perspiration.

Monsignor Paci prayed and sprinkled holy water at the opening of the mine as Signore James Gardner and Signore John Forester Rose, the mine owners, finally approached the desperate scene. Mr. Gardner seemed more sympathetic to the situation. He was a tall, handsome American, from Boston my father always spoke to us about.

Signore Rose had a stone face and wore his hair like a woman, down to his shoulders. He was English Papà said, and he seemed to be looking down his nose at everything. It was the first time I ever saw these two, wealthy men, both sons of the original mine owners. Eleven years prior, Signore Rose was held for ransom by desperate bandits, and he was never at ease without a bodyguard or two. Both of the mine owners wore bright-white, linen pants and shirts and had funny looking white shoes on their feet. Years later I learned they enjoyed playing the game of tennis together at Villa Lisetta, an enormous Victorian estate in town. The Rose and Gardner families were very close. Everyone knew that John Forester Rose had married Elizabeth Gardner, the sister of James Gardner. Occasionally, she would be seen with her husband's mother at the market, where people would stop and stare at the foreigners in their fine clothing.

I dropped my hand from Mama's skirt in order to get closer to the men. I wanted to hear what they were saying to each other. My heart was racing and my mind was frantic thinking about my poor Papà underneath the ground. I wanted to take a pick and shovel and start digging into the mine to try to save him and the others. *At least try,* I thought to myself.

The men, the owners, and the mine's manager, spoke in English and Italian. I only understood Sicilian, but I could make out a few Italian words.

"All dead... gas... explosion... fire... tragic... production... and other mines."

I put the pieces together trying to get an understanding of what was going on. Signore Rose wanted the other picconiere and carusi to get back to work on the other mines around the Colle Madore. Signore Modica gave a hand signal, and someone blew a whistle which told the sufatari to return to their mines.

I knew at that moment my life would change forever and I would never see my Papà's face again.

CHAPTER 2

NOVEMBER 22, 1876

LERCARA FRIDDI, SICILY

Eleven Years Before the Mine Explosion
John Rose is Captured by Bandits

John Rose's father, Mr. James Rose was in his study at Villa Lisetta. He was reviewing correspondence from London that had arrived in the day's mail. A tall, striking man in his early fifties with salt and pepper hair, the senior Rose had a commanding countenance. Oxford educated, James Rose was a successful banker who had inherited his father's sulfur mining business in Sicily.

"Sorry to disturb you, but a brigand just left this letter for you at the front door. I thought it might be important," the English butler announced. Thomas had been with the Rose family his entire life. Always dressed in formal attire, the sixty-five-year-old, balding butler and man Friday rarely left the estate unless he was needed to run errands.

The letter was in Sicilian. Written with pencil on brown paper a butcher would wrap meat in, some of the letters were printed, others in a script that was difficult to read unless one was native to the Sicilian language.

Rose summoned his housekeeper who could read, write, and speak enough English to communicate well with the members of the wealthy Rose family.

"Maria, what do you make of this?" Rose asked.

Maria, short and plump with her hair pulled back in a tight bun, read the letter. Her face went ashen, and she felt as if she would pass out. The butler brought the trembling woman to the security of a chair.

"My God, Signore Rose. The bandits have taken Signore John. They want money for his return," Maria gasped.

Rose's wife and daughter-in-law, Elizabeth, were in the parlor and scurried to the study after hearing the commotion.

"Read the entire letter for me, would you Maria? Thomas, please get her some water," Rose commanded.

"Signore James Rose. We have your son, John Forester Rose. He has not been harmed. For his safe return to you, we require twenty thousand British pounds. The money must be left in a box which will be at the base of the Colle Madore. Do not try to trap us, as your son will surely die."

"O, Dio mio, Signore," Maria gasped, invoking the name of God.

Elizabeth Gardner Rose, the kidnapped man's wife, a stunning, young woman with curly, brown hair stood in stunned silence. The elder Mrs. Rose, John's mother, showed no emotion but was incredulous.

"Who would do such a thing? James, summon the carabinieri at once. This is an outrage!" the elder Mrs. Rose bellowed.

Thomas took the Rose's fastest horse and made his way to carabinieri headquarters in the center of town. A short while later, Thomas, a squad of men, and the head of the carabinieri, Comandante Pietro Greco arrived at the Villa Lisetta.

Greco had a no-nonsense look on his rugged complexion. His men called the Comandante "Frenchy" behind his back due to his Norman-red hair and sky-blue eyes. Greco was in full, dark blue uniform which was modeled after the French Gendarmerie at the time. Greco proudly wore his gold medal of Italian independence in the center of his chest signifying his service during the Italian unification. He wore a bicorne, a two-cornered hat which gave him a look of elegance and authority.

"May I see the letter, Signore Rose?" Greco asked.

Greco read the note and inspected the paper and envelope for a while before commenting.

"I have some questions, please. Where was John Forester today?"

"He had a meeting with me at the bank and then he had planned to visit the sulfur mine," the senior Rose stated.

"Who accepted this letter, or was it placed in the post box?"

"I accepted the letter at the door," Thomas the butler announced.

"Please describe what the person looked like who handed you the letter."

"Well, he was short, I guess average size for a Sicilian. Very muscular as if he worked in the fields. I recall his hands were a bit soiled, and he had a beard and moustache. There was a scar that ran between his eyes. He smiled at me with a full set of teeth," Thomas answered.

"Thank you. Mr. Rose, may we talk privately?" Greco asked.

Rather than ask everyone to leave the study, Mr. Rose took Comandante Greco into the library on the first floor of the estate.

"Sir, to me this is clearly the work of the bandit Antonino Leone. He is a notorious criminal. It can be assumed that John Forester was overtaken on his way to the mine. Believe me when I tell you this is a great embarrassment for our citizens and our community, and all of Italy, but know there will be no witnesses to your son's abduction. The man your butler described is a lieutenant in Leone's brigade. His name is Giuseppe Esposito. He is from Alia, not very far from Lercara. Esposito is wanted for murder and extortion. I must tell you Antonino Leone is a vicious man who will not be merciful if you do not cooperate with his demands. He is also wanted for a number of other crimes, including murder. Esposito is bad into his soul. A vicious killer. Be guided by my words, please."

"Are you suggesting I pay this man?" Rose asked. The way he asked the question, his tone, told Greco payment was out of the question.

"Sir, I'm saying that if you think these men are not serious, and you do not give them what they want, they will slaughter your son like a lamb and think nothing of it."

"Comandante, if we succumb to these people we will be a target every day of our lives. I much prefer that we stand tall, stall, and give you and your men the opportunity to track these animals down and bring them to justice. I will meet with the mayor and prefect and demand they send reinforcements from Palermo for you. In the meantime, my banks cannot be used as a source of income to these bandits."

"As you wish, Mr. Rose. I must advise you that these hills and mountains are filled with hiding places, caves and such. Finding your son will not be impossible, but it is unlikely. Leone and his men know the countryside as you know your own villa."

"We have work to do, Comandante. Please help me find my boy."

CHAPTER 3

Back to the Mine Explosion

Walking back to town, everyone who was at the mine was in the state of shock.

One of the widows, who was the mother of one of my friends practically since birth, Carlo Panepinto, asked my Mama, "Now what? What do we do now? How will we feed these children?"

Mama replied, "We could barely feed them with our husbands working from dawn to dusk. I've given up praying." Mama looked down at me for a moment and looked away, the look on her face had a different anguish now. I was the eldest of the boys. Me, Aspanu Salerno, four years old, soon to be five, was now the man of the house. Maybe I could find some work to help my family.

Everyone stopped at the church to light a candle for the dead. I never felt comfortable inside that dark, mysterious place. Today was no exception. The sobbing continued, echoing off the high, mural-filled ceilings. The aroma of incense wafted through the church. Monsignor Paci was not around to help comfort the grieving widows. The priest was with Mayor Sartorio three blocks away having an afternoon aperitivo.

Soon, the list of names of those who perished would be posted in the town square so people could see if a friend or relative was gone in that sulfur mine.

After the sobs and wailing subsided inside the church, we began walking the few blocks back. Mama's eyes were puffy, almost closed, her face streaked with tears mixed with the dust from the area around the mines. She remained erect as she walked so as not to show any signs of weakness. The strength of a good Sicilian woman was stronger than ten horses, Papà used to say. Papà also said to us all, 'Fa a facci cuntenta,' go with a happy face, so no one would try to take advantage of us. Mama listened well, reacting to the worst situation of her life with style and grace.

Once inside our house, Mama tended to the goat we had. Lena, the goat, provided milk for all of the children in the house, eating the hay and oats and bushes we would gather to help her make her milk. Two, red, plump gaddini ran around the house but stayed close by. They came into the house in the evening. If they wandered too far, they would surely wind up in someone's pot. We needed their eggs to survive…especially now that Papà was gone.

I already missed Papà terribly. My stomach always ached from constant hunger, but now there was a different pang. An emptiness that I never knew could be. Papà always came home by six-thirty in the evening. He would walk through the door, and the house would suddenly smell of sulfur. Not an especially foul odor, but something that resembled chemicals. Some people would say rotten eggs or farts. To me, it was just something I was used to. Even after Mama would draw a bath for Papà, he still smelled of sulfur. It was in his skin I suppose, or in his internal organs. We could smell it on his breath when he hugged us and kissed us goodnight. The aroma of sulfur would last with us for at least a few minutes. He didn't take a bath every night, and there were times he smelled foul from working but just collapsed in his bed when he had returned from the mines. Mama and Papà's bed was right next to where all the children slept. Sometimes his smell made me gag a bit, and sometimes I liked it. Now I will miss it forever.

We all cried ourselves to sleep that night. Mama gave me that quick look again then she suddenly looked away, her gaze moving rapidly toward the small statue of Santa Barbara on the small corner table Papà had made by hand.

By early morning, we were all doing our chores. By eleven, the sun would scorch the ground with a vengeance. By one, it was unbearable to work outside. I thought of the heat down in the mines and how terrible that must have been for Papà. Anyway, life had to go on, and I needed to find food for the chickens and the goat. I ate a small piece of stale bread, three olives, and a cup of goat's milk, and prepared to leave the house.

I heard Signora Panepinto calling my mother's name and whistling her familiar tune to announce her arrival. Carlo called out my name. He came to visit and do his chores with me. The Panepintos also lived on Via Cimò, just up a slight incline from us.

"Okay, boys, leave us to talk alone, please. Go do your chores," Signora Panepinto said. Her voice was serious. Of course, it was the day before that she also lost her husband and the family breadwinner.

"Make sure they are not listening," Mama warned.

"Maria," Carlo's mother said, "I know it's early to discuss what to do now that our men are gone, but we have to face the facts. How will we put food on the table?"

"In this town, there are only two ways left my dear, Elvira. Sell yourself to the miners in that brothel on Via Ortigia, or sell our sons to the picconieri."

"The soccorso di morti? The rescue from death?

"You know as well as I do what happens to the carusi in those mines. You've heard the awful stories of how some of those picconieri treat the boys. You've seen as I have the horrible way carusi are disfigured and the early deaths from all those diseases. Every week, that stupid priest buries at least one carusi, never mind the accidents that swallow them whole by the dozens into the earth," Elvira lamented.

"I would rather slit my own throat than become a buttana. A whore. We have our other children to think about. They need food to live. I don't think I can feed them for more than two weeks with what little food I can scrape together. I don't want to watch their bellies bloat as they starve to death," Maria stated.

"Our boys will only be five years old soon. They are still babies. Carlo still wets his bed sometimes. What a terrible predicament we have found ourselves in," Elvira added.

"Listen to me, my dear friend, our boys are smart; we must keep them together so Aspanu and Carlo watch after each other. In time, they will grow and become picconieri themselves as their fathers and grandfathers were. We must sell them together or not at all! I don't see that we have a choice in the matter," Maria Salerno said.

It was the only thing to do, the only practical solution in the face of starvation.

Suddenly a loud knocking on the front door startled the two, grieving women.

CHAPTER 4

More on the Kidnapping from

Eleven Years Earlier

November, 1876

In one of the many natural caves around the Colle Madore, Antonino Leone, Giuseppe Esposito, and four of their crew of bandits held John Forester Rose captive.

The Colle Madore is the largest hill in the countryside outside Lercara Friddi. The natural sulfur deposits in the area brought the ancient Sicani people to settle here in 800 B.C. The Sicani tribe built a foundry using the sulfur for fuel and medicinal purposes. Now bandits held a wealthy, young businessman prisoner on the same hillside that had made his family rich.

The young Mr. Rose's wavy, brown hair, now matted from perspiration, and his two-day, scruffy beard, was very much unlike how the always meticulously groomed, nattily dressed, twenty-two-year old heir to the Rose family fortune presented himself.

John Forester Rose, newly wed within the last eight months to Elizabeth Gardner, enjoyed the finer things in life, and he worked hard to deserve them. John's father was not one who spoiled his children, although the elder Rose's influence made things easy enough for them to succeed. John and his siblings were expected to work hard from an early age.

John F. Rose now ran the mining end of the family business while becoming fluent in French, Italian, and Sicilian. The French were the biggest consumers of sulfur in the world after the English, and knowing the French language gave the Gardner-Rose Company an advantage in the marketplace.

Now, he was trapped by a band of notorious and dangerous gangsters who couldn't care less if they killed him or freed him.

"So, your father now has his instructions. Twenty thousand pounds and you will be returned unharmed." Leone laughed. "A bit dirty and smelly but at least in one piece. Of course, your Papà called the carabinieri, who are as useless as a tit-less cow. We have eyes and ears everywhere in these mountain towns, so we know their every move. But I'm concerned for you, Signore Rose," Leone stated.

"Concerned? Is that why you have my legs tied and my wrists bound together? Maybe I should be concerned for you and your men. My father will use all his resources to find you," Rose replied.

"You English have a way of pretending you are not afraid. Is it arrogance or theatre? I find either to be admirable. We can learn from you," Leone countered.

"Maybe we should have asked for forty thousand British pounds from those blood suckers, Anto," Esposito blurted.

"Maybe next time we will, if we take his wife or one of his children, if he ever has any with that pretty, American wife," Leone responded. Leone made a slinky shape of the outline of a woman's shape with his hands. John Forester Rose found the gesture repugnant.

"This is why my father will not pay your ransom. He realizes we will always be a mark and there will never be an end to this with your kind. Extortion is not something the Rose family is unfamiliar with."

"So, then he will lose a son." Esposito offered. The robber picked at his teeth with a piece of wood he had whittled.

Leone loosened the rope binding Rose's hands. The bandit offered John a drink of wine from a lambskin wine pouch, some bread, and pecorino cheese. The food was wrapped in an oil-stained, red and black kerchief.

"I'm sorry our hospitality does not afford the elegance you are used to, Signore Rose, but under the circumstances..."

Leone gestured with his hand to indicate the cave.

Leone continued. "Tonight, it will be cold in here. That's our typical Sicilian weather in November, still warm in the day and stingingly cold at night. We have only a light blanket for you," Leone said.

"Anto, why are you thinking about his comfort? To hell with him and his whole rotten family. Do you think for one minute they give two shits about the surfarari? Does the Rose or Gardner family care at all about those poor slave carusi? All they care about is their money. How many tons of this devil's gold can they pull from the earth on the backs of our Sicilian brothers and sisters? I say we take the money and cut his throat anyway, just for practice," Esposito declared. He glared at the emotionless John Forester Rose through his diatribe.

Rose felt a tightening in his stomach and sphincter.

Leone looked at his ranting lieutenant and showed nothing on his face that would indicate agreement or otherwise.

"Let's see what tomorrow brings. If we hear nothing from his father, we will send another letter. I have plenty of paper and a good pencil if his estimable father wants to prolong this game of cat and mouse," Leone replied.

CHAPTER 5

Back to the Explosion

Eleven Years After Kidnapping

Elvira Panepinto stepped away so Maria Salerno could answer the knocking on her front door.

In the doorway stood a young man, not too much younger than the women, obviously a surfararu by the size of his hands and the sharp aroma of sulfur about him. He held a brown miners cap in his hands, his head was down as if he was inspecting his bare feet.

The two new widows, both dressed in traditional black dresses and scarves for mourning waited for the young man to speak. After a long pause, it was evident he would not engage the women.

"Excuse me, signore, but do you have the right house? Have you come to pay your respects to my husband?" Maria queried.

"I am sorry for your loss, signora, for both of you. I knew both of your husbands only in passing and I...I'm sorry that..."

"I cannot invite you in, signore, as there is no man of the house present, but I will bring you a glass of wine in a moment. Please wait here."

Maria closed the door and shrugged her shoulders to Elvira.

"I've never seen him before. I have no idea why he is here either," Elvira said.

"He should have brought his wife along to be respectful. Let's bring this wine to him and be hospitable and see what he wants."

"That's if he will even talk," Elvira added.

As Maria opened the door one of the hens ran from the house looking for the other hen. No one noticed.

The front of the small house was paved with beige and white sandstone and dirt. Shade from an adjacent, larger home gave a momentary reprieve from the sun, which would relentlessly bake the house within the hour.

"Thank you, signora. My wife would have joined me to visit, but she had our first baby yesterday, and she is not feeling too well," the man said. He accepted the small glass of wine and brought it to his dry, cracked lips.

"Ah, lu signuri li benedica, God bless them both," Maria said. She was relieved the man was married and a father, and he understood the traditional and respectful roles between men and women.

"The baby was born on a day when so many died. This is God's way of replacing one of the souls," Elvira added.

"Yes…again, I mourn your terrible loss, both of you," the man said again awkwardly.

The widows stood next to each other, like a black, lace wall, waiting for something else to be said. Maria heard her husband's voice with a warning, 'a fish dies by its open mouth.' She was determined to listen before she spoke again. It was not Elvira's place to speak while on her friend's property.

After another uncomfortable time, the man cleared his throat and finally spoke.

"Excuse me, my name is Domenico Alia. I am a surfararu at the Gardner-Rose mine. I was in another mine when the explosion and cave in occurred yesterday. I have been a picconiere for the last four years, before that, I was a carusu until I was seventeen. I am from Marineo, not here, not from Lercara. But we live here now, me, my wife, and my son, to be close to the mines," Domenico uttered.

The women remained silent.

Maria noticed Domenico's left shoulder was lower than his right shoulder, and he had a small hunch to his back. His right arm was also longer than his left arm. Domenico was not tall, not short, but powerfully built.

"I'm sorry to come here on the day after the tragedy, but Sunday is my only day off from the mines. I wanted to talk to you both about your sons."

Still silence from Maria and Elvira.

"I am in need of two carusi to help me with my work. Please…please understand I am a good man. I was a carusu myself and I know what some of these men do with the boys. How they beat them and treat them badly…and other things. I would never do that to your boys, as God as my witness."

Maria took a step closer to Domenico. It was time she spoke.

"Signore Alia, what makes you think our boys will work in those wretched mines?" Maria asked.

"Forgive me, signora. You have lost your husband, and times are bad. You have mouths to feed. Unless there are other jobs available for young boys, I thought you would want to place your sons with a good man. A man who respects a dead miner's son. If I have said anything to offend you..."

"No...No, Signore Alia. You have not offended. This is all just a bit too much to take after yesterday," Elvira offered.

"I am very sorry. I can only wait a few days and borrow two carusi from a friend, but I will need to find my own help. I have borrowed money from my father-in-law for the soccorso di morti. I am willing to pay three hundred lire per boy. That is top dollar. But I must warn you, many carusi perished yesterday. There will be carusi coming from other towns for work when word gets around. The gabbeloto still demands his tally. I advise you, think things over and decide soon. With all respect, signora," Domenico said.

"How long were you a carusu, Signore Alia?" Maria asked.

"From six-years old until I was seventeen. Eleven years, signora. In the mines of Marineo."

"Why were you a carusu?"

"My father left us. I was the oldest son."

"And your child now? Is he a masculine child?" Maria asked.

"Yes, signora."

"Would you want your son to be a carusu, Signore Alia?"

"No, signora. Not as long as there in breath in my body. It is not a good life for a boy. As long as I can provide for my family I will do whatever I can to keep my son out of the mine. But, if God takes me...we must do what we have to do in order to survive, signora."

Maria looked at Domenico and then at Elvira.

"We will discuss this together after mass today. How can we find you, Signore Alia?"

CHAPTER 6

"Pardon me, Mr. Rose, but another letter has arrived," Thomas announced.   Rose was engrossed with business documents on the large, mahogany desk in his study.

Thomas took the initiative to bring Maria the housekeeper into the study to translate the letter.

"Thomas, how was this letter delivered?" Rose asked.

"A young boy delivered it to the carabinieri that are guarding the Villa, sir. They are questioning the boy now, but he seems dim-witted, sir. The Comandante has already been sent for," Thomas replied.

"That will be all, Maria. The Comandante will be here directly. He can translate for me," Rose muttered.

Within minutes, Greco arrived at the estate with his contingency of carabinieri and elegant officers in tow.

"Have you opened the letter, Signore Rose?" Greco asked.

"No, I haven't. We decided to wait for you. The fewer people that are aware of these things, the better, I believe."

"Yes, that is sound judgment."

Rose handed Greco the letter which was wrapped in the same butcher paper on which the first letter had been written.

Mr. James Rose, Greco, and two of the Comandante's men were left in the study.

Greco read the letter aloud.

"Signore Rose. This is a warning to you. Do not trifle with me. By now, your puppet Greco has told you who I am. Above all, I am a man who demands respect. If the money is not in the box by today at dusk, I will take your no reply as an insult. You are warned." Greco handed the letter over to his captain and continued.

"And he had the gall to sign the letter with a large L," Greco seethed.

"How is your search for Leone going, Comandante?" Mr. Rose asked.

"We have two hundred police and militia covering the hills and surrounding towns. More than half are from Palermo, sent by your friend from Rome, the Minister of the Interior, Giovanni Nicotera. My instructions are very clear from Signore Nicotera. I am to do whatever is necessary to find John Forester Rose. We are working around the clock, Signore. Every cave and every crevice will be inspected. My men have orders to shoot to kill the kidnappers if necessary."

"Have you had any indication so far, any evidence or approximate whereabouts on where this bandit is hiding?"

"Signore, these hills are vast. There are so many caves and hiding places that our job would be difficult with even two thousand men. For all we know, he is being held up meters from here in a house. We are checking the caves first because that is how Leone has operated in the past. I must be frank with you Signore, the people of this area, in the whole of Sicily for that matter, while upset with what has happened to your family, they see, hear, and say nothing," Greco exclaimed.

"I suppose reward money would not help?" Rose queried.

Greco grimaced and nodded in the negative. "What value does a man put on his own life? Any cooperation with the authorities would be met with certain death for the man who talks and for his entire family. We are dealing with a people who have been conquered so many times, I could fill a sheet of paper. From the Phoenicians, the Greeks, Romans, French, Spanish, Arabs. The blood of the Sicilians is a mixture like no other in the world. They have learned their lessons well, Mr. Rose. To them, you are yet another conquering army."

"That's nonsense, Signore Greco. We are simply businessmen seeking profit and growth. And what of the jobs we give these starving people? At least they have work to support themselves. We couldn't care less about taking over Sicily or any other place for that matter," Rose said.

"With all due respect sir, the British have a reputation that precedes them. Let us just stay with what we know for the moment. As

I advised you yesterday, pay the money for your son's life. Put it behind you, then take the necessary precautions not to become a victim again."

"This is what my son's mother and his wife want. They have begged me to pay this low-life, and I say the same to you as I said to them. The Rose family will not negotiate with murderers and thieves. My only regret is that I did not see this coming from this scum. I should have taken more prudent precautions to protect my family. I will tell you here and now that my partner, Mr. Gardner, is making plans with private concerns in America to protect our interests and our families' lives in this God-forsaken town going forward. Hear me well, Comandante, we will track these men down and kill them if my son is harmed. For now, you best go and find John, or I will see to it that you will be drummed out of your organization in disgrace," Rose ranted.

Rose then called for his butler to see the comandante and his men to the door.

Louis Romano   Carusi: The Shame of Sicily

CHAPTER 7

The main church in Lercara Friddi overlooks the largest piazza in the center of town...Chiesa Parrocchiale Maria Ss. Della Neve, at the Piazza Duomo. Eight smaller churches in town illustrate the Roman Catholic influence of the Lecaresi.

When a catastrophe like the explosion and collapse of the Gardner-Rose Company mine occurs, the entire town makes for Maria Della Neve. This Sunday was a demonstration of the Lecaresi religiosity. Or was it the Sicilian superstitions that filled the chairs?

The painted white, plaster-over-stone church was built high atop a long set of dark, stone steps. Three towers loomed over the main entrance's green door, where the procession of the widows and mothers would begin. Over the main entrance in bold, black, print, the Latin words, *venite adoremus*, come let us worship, beckons the faithful.

The common expression of sorrow, 'there for the grace of God, go I' made every man and woman inside the church bless themselves multiple times as the procession passed where they sat. Some subtly spit through their fingers to ward off the evil eye as the priest swung the incense censer on its single chain to purify the gold-appointed, marble altar, which was built with the church in 1760.

Nearly everyone in the church, at least those born in Lercara Friddi, were baptized at the font in the back of the church. Altars to a variety of saints and Madonna's, on either side of the main aisle, encourage believers to pray to their select and favorite icons. In the middle of the church there is an entrance which leads to a crypt of the dead clergy who have served the community.

The widows and mothers of the dead picconieri and carusi, in their long, black dresses and black, cloth head covers, lined up outside on the church steps behind Monsignor Paci for the morning mass. The ceremony wasn't an official funeral mass, per se, but a mass said for the repose of the souls of the newly departed.

Contribution baskets were sent down each row a number of times during the mass with the same results. They all returned empty. There was not enough lire to buy food to feed babies, never mind keeping the fat priests in the style in which they had become accustomed.

Maria Salerno and Elvira Panepinto were among the many mourners who insisted their children be present and well behaved in the church for this sacred mass.

Aspanu and Carlo busied themselves trying to count the ten, red, marble columns from the quarries of the nearby town of Castronovo. Aspanu could count to ten, but Carlo became mixed up after five.

The boys took seats inside the church while their mothers waited outside. The women lined up on the church steps, some still wailing, awaiting the procession to move forward.

From behind Maria and Elvira, an older woman, who lost two grown sons and her husband the day before, spoke so those around her could hear.

"Look how God stepped on our families? Wasn't life hard enough for us? Now this? What did we do to deserve this penance? Where is this God they tell us to pray to?"

"God gives you only as much as you can bear," another voice said.

"After this day, I will spit when I hear the word Jesus or Lord or God," another said.

"You dare to blaspheme on the steps of this holy church? Are you not worried about what other affliction can be set upon us? Shame on you all," Elvira blurted.

"Easy for you to say. You still have choices. You are still young, you can go to America, you can meet another man and your womb can produce another child. You can make ends meet, but we here are finished. All that's left for us to do is to starve," the first woman said.

Maria pulled back the veil in front of her face, turned on her heels, and addressed the lamenting women.

"Go to America? With what and how? Now we must send our sons into the sulfur mines to put bread on the table? Give up the health and happiness of one child in order to feed the others? This is a choice? What level of hell are we choosing, you stupid women? Having no faith in the Lord is siding with the devil. Shame on you all."

From the left tower, as if on cue from a higher power, the church bell let out a single bong, signaling the procession to start into the packed church. Every ten seconds, another bong was rung until all of the black-draped mourners took their seats at the front of the church. The dramatic effect of the bell set the tone for the morbid proceedings, capped off by the choir singing *Ave Maria*, a tear-jerking hymn on a good day.

Three priests said the lengthy Latin high mass. In the seats, the sound of stomachs rumbling from hunger could be heard during the solemn consecration of the host. The fast was imposed by the church. No one could receive the body of Christ in the symbolic consecration while there was food in their stomach. In some cases, the communion host was as much breakfast as the faithful were going to eat this day.

In his homily, Monsignor Paci pulled at the heart strings of the worshipers, warning more fervent prayer and good works, plus generosity to the church, will help the Lecaresi to be led into heaven and avoid future catastrophe. A final basket appeal after the Monsignor's heartfelt homily still did not reap donations.

After the mass was finished and a sea of tears were shed for those killed in the Gardner-Rose mine accident, Maria and Elvira stopped in the piazza to chat with an old friend from their school days, Carmela Miceli.

Carmela was dressed in the traditional mourning dress and veil, her young daughter standing next to her, her head clinging to her mother's breast.

"You too, Carmela? Your husband, too?" Maria asked.

"Yes, ladies. And my seven-year old son, Pino, as well. They worked together as father and son."

"What a pity for you and your daughter. I cannot believe she has grown into a young woman. We haven't seen you in so long, Carmela," Elvira added.

"Yes. She will be twelve years old soon, and already budding into a young lady. She is all I have left now. We are faced with this terrible tragedy, and our lives will now change for the worse. My daughter will soon leave school and work outside the house her father and I built," Carmela said through trembling lips.

The young girl, also in a black funeral dress, but without the veil, was cried out of tears. She wore a black, cloth, kerchief on top of her head. Both of the girl's eye sockets were black as coal, and she appeared to be in a different world, her eyes cast down to the ground with no response to the outside world.

"What is your name, little one?" Maria asked.

No response from the girl who continued to stare as if in a trance.

Her mother finally replied, "Nina. Her name is Nina, and she hasn't spoken since yesterday. Doctor Giordano said she is in a state of shock. Who knows when she will return to normal?"

Carmela continued; "And what about your families? What will you do now?"

"We both have sons. Just a bit younger than your Nina. I have Aspanu, and Elvira has her son, Carlo. Just this morning a picconiere came to my house to offer the soccorso di morti for our sons to work as carusi," Maria informed.

"Two more of our boys, destined to the treachery of those mine owners. If the fumes don't kill them, the explosions will. If they escape those horrors then the parasites eat them from the inside slowly. My poor boy was already seeing Doctor Giordano for the organisms growing inside his young body. Maybe God spared him a worse death yesterday," Carmela lamented.

CHAPTER 8

Aspanu and Carlo ran ahead of their mothers, back to Via Cimò. The boys had enough stored energy to pull the train from Lercara Bassa, where the train station is at the base of Lercara Friddi, all the way to Palermo. Sitting in the church for so long made the boys want to run and play. Aspanu and Carlo had been looking around the church at the paintings and murals, trying to understand the story behind each scene, wondering what all the ceremony was. The statues high up on the outside of the church and scattered around the interior added to the dark mystery behind the religion. Aspanu knew the gathering had to do with his father being dead, but Carlo seemed not to grasp the reason why everyone was somber and quiet.

Maria and Elvira walked slowly, as the heat from the late morning sun seemed to bake them even more in their mourning dresses.

"Those women on the steps of the church were very bitter. They should be careful with what they say. God will punish them for even thinking such evil thoughts," Elvira declared.

"I felt badly about being strong on them. I think I was just overcome by everything that was going on. Who am I to judge? I will admit that my own thoughts have brought me to such despair," Maria answered.

"Maria, when I look at my poor son, I simply cannot see him going down into those mines all day, working like an animal with strangers who couldn't care less about him."

"Carrying those baskets, day after day, heavy with sulfur, until their backs are deformed. This is not a life my dear husband and I wanted for Aspanu. I want to vomit at the thought of him being used like a slave," Maria said. She stopped walking, holding her stomach as if she was truly going to be sick.

"And that parasite disease that older woman mentioned. My husband spoke of it. The miners and the carusi get the disease from the cracks in their bare feet. My God almighty, what is this hell we will send our boys into?" Elvira questioned.

"And if we decided to take his offer, how long will it take us to pay back the picconieri... this Signore Alia?" Maria asked.

"I have heard of carusi who worked from five or six years old until they were fifteen, maybe older. Putting our sons underground that long is like a punishment, maybe a death sentence, God forbid. They are innocent babies, Maria, but what other choice will we have? At least for a while we will be able feed our families with the money Signore Alia gives us."

"And do we trust him that he will not beat our boys if they are not working as hard as they should? We will know nothing about what goes on in that mine? What if one of the other picconieri grabs them in the dark? Oh my God!!!" Maria shouted.

"Maria...once we accept the soccorso di morti, they are no longer our sons from dawn to dusk. Alia will own them. We are selling the boys to him. Our babies become his property; that is the law."

"I need time to sort this out. How can we put our trust into Signore Alia so soon after our husbands were just killed? I think we should look at any other way but this," Maria cried.

"You heard Signore Alia as well as I did. Soon there may not be an opening. Then what we do? We need to decide here and now what we will do. Either way, we will keep those two boys together," Elvira insisted.

Maria had stored some dried macaroni in the nearly barren cupboard. She made a sauce of tomatoes, beans, and basil which she'd picked from her garden in the rear of her house. When the pot boiled and the macaroni was ready, the sauce was mixed into it, filling the small house with a familiar fragrance.

The children did not need to be called. They were always hungry and the rustling of pots and pans along with the aroma of the food, naturally brought them to the table. Aspanu, now the eldest, was served before his siblings. Before the accident, Papà was always served first. This made Aspanu sad enough to drop a few tears onto the table. Mama and the other kids didn't notice as they were fixated on dealing with their own grumbling stomachs.

Louis Romano   Carusi: The Shame of Sicily

CHAPTER 9

After fifteen days, now into December, there was no sign of John Forester Rose.   Antonino Leone, the treacherous bandit of Western Sicily, moved his weary captive sometimes two or three times a day to avoid his pursuers.

Comandante Greco asked for an immediate meeting at Villa Lisetta to review new information on the kidnapping with Mr. and Mrs. Rose and John Forester Rose's wife, Elizabeth Gardner-Rose.

It was an unseasonably warm day for late November. Mr. Rose moved the meeting to the back of the house where a large, linen-covered table, and stone benches adorned with pastel-painted flowers, awaited. Refreshments and finger sandwiches, otherwise unknown in Sicily, were served by Thomas and his staff.

"Thank you for seeing me and for your generous hospitality," Greco began. *These people have no idea how to eat,* he thought to himself.

"We have received a third letter from Leone, left on the steps of our headquarters, early this morning.   The letter has threatened to send one or both of your son's ears to you if the ransom is not paid immediately," Greco blurted.

"Comandante, I'm sure you realize that my son has been in the clutches of this so-called bandit, Leone, for a half month. Frankly, we are all disappointed in your results," Mr. Rose asserted.

"Signore Rose, our Minister of the Interior in Rome, Giovanni Nicotera, has sent twenty-five hundred men to add to our local forces to assist in finding your son. This case has become a national embarrassment to our government. I am certain your diplomats are exerting pressure in Rome. Frankly, we are doing our best to find your son. We have offered a reward of fifty thousand lire, an enormous sum, for anonymous information, to all the farmers and laborers. In addition, we have a bounty, dead or alive, for Leone and Esposito and his band of gangsters. Our men are working around the clock, and we have not one lead to go on. This Leone is skilled at what he does, and I again implore you to negotiate a payment. Surely, twenty thousand pounds is an extraordinary amount of ransom to pay, Mr. Rose, but Sicilians are a people who are used to negotiating everything. Perhaps a lesser amount may interest Leone and his men," Greco offered.

"And how do you propose we make this offer, Comandante? It's laughable you cannot find this devil for weeks but an offer of money will find its way into the hills by some Sicilian magic. That is preposterous!" Rose shouted.

Greco was about to answer when Elizabeth Gardner-Rose stood from her chair. She had been silent on her husband's kidnapping until now. After two weeks, the beautiful, young woman had large, dark bags around her eyes even her best, French makeup could not mask.

"I've had just about enough of this. Clearly this society, with its secrets and superstitions, has a way of communicating with Leone. I am not interested in how it's done, or who will kill whom if they talk. Nor do I want to hear which saint will return my John to me. I'm interested in the safety of my husband. I'm sure he is still alive. Leone has only one bargaining chip, and that is my husband."

Elizabeth continued, putting her hand up to stop any response from Greco or her father-in-law.

"Benjamin Gardner came to Sicily, appointed by President John Quincy Adams, as diplomatic consul to this island in 1825. He decided to begin his sulfur mining business with my husband's family. They selected, with a great investment to start their mine in this town, Lercara Friddi, to make their fortune. I rue the day that Benjamin ever left Boston, and I curse the day his friend and lawyer, the great Daniel Webster put his name up as a recommendation to President Adams. However, here we are, faced with a business problem. Yes, this is a business problem, gentleman, and as I see it, in this hellish place, in this hellish world, a cost of doing business. Enough of this stalling and bluffing. Comandante, I have the funds that Leone wants. What are you proposing?"

The elder Mrs. Rose beamed with pride at her daughter-in-law's courage. Mr. Rose was dumbfounded a woman would be so bold. Greco was taken aback by the young, diminutive woman's self-assured soliloquy. He paused for a moment before he replied.

Greco kept his attention on Mr. Rose.

"I suggest that we offer five thousand pounds, paid in the manner in which…."

"Comandante Greco, you will please address me and not my father-in-law. It may be difficult for you to deal with a woman on this level but you haven't a choice in the matter. I am Mrs. John Forester Rose, and he is my responsibility. I just explained to you I am willing to pay Leone for my husband's safe return. Ears and all," Elizabeth declared.

"Pardon me, Mrs. Rose. I suggest we offer five thousand pounds. I will get the word to the farmers and laborers immediately. Leone will have this information quickly and…"

Elizabeth interrupted. "…and you will let him know I will be dealing with him and not anyone else. Let him know I also had family who were rebels…Paul Revere, for one, and several others who fought the British for our independence. I want him to know that information, Signore Greco. I want him to know there is a strength of will I inherited from my ancestors."

The independence remark was a bit unsettling for Mr. Rose but he understood Elizabeth's negotiating tactic.

CHAPTER 10

Maria and Elvira asked family members to sit with their children for a while. They were in search of the address where Domenico Alia told them he lived on Via Friddi, near the sulfur mine. The walk took the better part of thirty minutes from Via Cimò much of the way dusty and unpaved. Their black clothing had a film of dust which seemed to turn their mourning dresses gray.

The widows walked in silence, their thoughts weighing heavily on their hearts.

Alia's home was a small, ramshackle house, with a small vegetable garden on the side that grew squash, zucchini, and few herbs. Most of Lercara Friddi's vegetables came from farms outside the town limits. A large tree was already full of nearly ripe figs, and a peach tree had substantial, ready-to-pick fruit. Tomato plant sticks stood at attention as a second crop he and his wife depended upon for sustenance for the fall and winter months. A few chickens pecked at the ground for bits of feed which were sprinkled about.

A small dog announced the widows' arrival with an incessant barking while it wagged its tail, indicating he was friendlier than a guard dog.

Domenico Alia opened the front door. He was dressed in brown, gabardine pants and a short-sleeved farmer's shirt with perspiration stains, indicating he did not have a day of complete rest. His young, wide-eyed wife, looking thin and rinsed out, was caressing their baby son in her arms. She wore a peasant's dress. Neither of the Alias wore shoes.

"Signore Alia, we hope we are not intruding," Maria announced.

"Not at all, signora. Please come in. Welcome to our home," Alia responded. His wife smiled uncomfortably.

The women found the interior of the Alia's home much like their own. One large bed, with an iron support and wooden boards around it.

The mattress was filled with straw. A small, black, wood burning stove, a few wooden cupboards, a dark, tattered chair, a basin to wash themselves and to wash laundry, and a hand-made, clothing closet was their entirety of their creature comforts. Water was brought into the house from fountains around town in large, earthenware bummulu, jars. And, of course, a table with wooden statues honoring Our Lady of Constantinople and Santa Barbara. A few votive candles burned, giving a sweet smell to the home.

Alia's wife put up a small macchinetta, a coffee maker, with her one hand while she held the baby in the other.

"Thank-you both for coming. This is my wife, Rosalia. She knows of my visit to your home this morning."

Maria and Elvira both smiled through their sadness while offering blessings to the baby. Elvira produced a small, miraculous medal as a gift for God's blessings on the child.

After a few pleasantries were made, they got to the business at hand.

Maria began the discussion: "Signore Alia, this is very difficult for us both. We are faced with a decision we never dreamed would befall us. Without our husbands to provide for our families, we cannot feed our children. Even with the small gardens we grow, it will not be possible for us to make ends meet. We would like to hear more about your offer of soccorso di morti to rescue and sustain us."

"I will tell you again, signora. I am a good man. I will not abuse your boys in any way. I am aware they are quite young, but I will train them to work as carusi for me. I have a daily quota to make for the gabbelloto. I will depend upon the boys to help bring the sulfur to the surface and into the calcaroni. If they slack off, I will reprimand them, but not in a brutal way as some picconieri do," Alia stated.

"We hear terrible stories about some picconieri who beat the carusi and do other unthinkable things to them. This we cannot abide, as you may well understand. Once you take them, how will we ever know…?" Elvira began to ask before she choked up and the tears fell from her eyes like a spring torrent.

"Signora Panepinto, Signora Salerno, I place my hand on the heart of my son and swear by God these awful things will never happen to your boys under my watch. I will not trick you. I must tell you, the work is very difficult. They will not enjoy playing as little boys want. They will work long hours with a short afternoon break. These are difficult times, and I wish you had other choices but we find ourselves...well, we all find ourselves trapped."

"They will come home to us each evening, correct?" Maria asked.

"Yes, of course. There are some carusi who are forced to sleep in the mines. They are usually orphans, or their families live in other towns, too far to walk home each evening. This is not the case with your dear boys. They will come home each and every night and be home all day Sunday. They will be exhausted from the day of labor and likely want to eat and sleep before beginning again at six the next morning."

"And their pay, Signore? They are paid daily?" Elvira asked.

"They are paid weekly. Mostly all of their pay is returned to me to pay off the soccorso di morti. A small sum will be given to them to return to you to help the household," Alia noted.

"Tell us again what the payment to us will be?" Elvira asked. Her jaw was clenched so as to prevent another stream of tears.

"I am prepared to offer two hundred and fifty lire for each boy. I promise to keep the boys together as we discussed."

"I will accept nothing less than three hundred lire. Signora Salerno agrees with this amount as well."

"Signora, that is unreasonable. Ask around for yourself. As I told you, I have borrowed this money from Rosalia's father and must pay him back over time. Most picconieri offer one hundred fifty, two hundred lire at the top. Besides, the more that is paid, the longer the time your boys will be in the mines as carusi. Perhaps, after a while, maybe four or five years at the earliest, they can become picconieri themselves and make more of a salary. What is more important is they will be treated well by me. As well as can be expected doing this daily labor."

Rosalia Alia served the coffee with their scarce sugar and a few baked biscuits.

"You are very nice, Signora, thank you," Maria whispered.

The young woman smiled slightly, her eyes downcast to avoid looking into the faces of these desperate widows.

Elvira never took her eyes from Domenico. She was looking for a sign of dishonesty, but she could not see any. He seemed reasonable and truthful.

"And when will you expect them to start work?" Elvira asked.

"There are other carusi coming into town tomorrow. If I have your commitment, I would expect both your sons to begin the day after tomorrow."

"They will have one more day to be little boys before they become slaves to the mines," Maria blurted.

"Signora, forgive me, but we are all slaves to the mine owners. This is our lot in life. I wish things were different for us all," Alia declared.

"We are both ready to make that commitment to you, Signore Alia. We are putting our trust in you as a man and a father," Maria replied. Her jaw trembled with grief.

"It is agreed then. Tomorrow, after work, I will come to your homes with the lire. They both must be at the Gardner-Rose mine Tuesday morning before the whistle at six. Please cut their hair as short as possible. That is for their own safety...for cleanliness. If they have a tight cap for their heads, that will also serve them well."

CHAPTER 11

Antonino Leone, after moving his captive from cave to cave in the Colle Madore area, decided the militia and army were getting a bit too close for comfort. Like a chess board, Leone had to be cautious about each move he made, lest he found himself at the end of a rope or standing blindfolded before a firing squad for kidnapping.

With the help of a friendly farmer, who was more interested in taking the fistful of lire offered by Leone and Esposito than helping the hated authorities, the bound and gagged John Forester Rose was concealed under some feed hay in a mule-driven cart.

The new hiding place was now a safe house well outside of Lercara Friddi, closer to the town of Marineo. One of Leone's loyal soldiers, who would kill or die for the bandit, drove the wagon while Leone, Esposito, and the rest of the gang of bandits followed 2 km behind. Leone gave his captive enough wine to help him fall into a sound sleep, aided by the rocking movement of the cart.

At one point during the move, at the Lercara Friddi town line, a group of sixteen soldiers, searching for John Forester Rose, came upon the mule cart, offering pleasantries as they passed the small wagon driven by the Leone associate. John Forester, in his wine induced sleep, had no idea that his freedom just happened to ride by him on dark stallions.

The cart arrived at the safe house in the hills, a short while before Leone and his crew of bandits. It was nine o'clock in the evening, perfect timing for a dinner of homemade spaghetti with tomato sauce and freshly-slaughtered, roasted lamb, cooked by a cousin of Leone and her husband.

John Forester was released from his bindings and allowed to partake in the delicious food and wine, but not at the table with the others. The young heir was locked in an old livestock room at the back of the dilapidated house, alone, with just one, small, votive candle for light.

Leone ate as if it were his last meal on earth, savoring the food on which he was raised...peasant fare in the mountains of Western Sicily. Leone addressed his cousins husband while they were all eating around the table.

"Oh, Davide, tell me what they are saying about me. Am I in the newspapers?" Leone laughed. He was always interested in what was being said about him, either truth or lore.

"Cugino, I can tell you, yes, I've seen the newspapers with your image, but like most of us around here, I never learned to read. I can't tell you exactly what the newspaper is saying, but the word scoundrel, robber, bandit, and other nice names are on the lips of the bosses. But, the ordinary people worship you because you are what they want to be. A man of his own mind using his balls to get what he wants. Maybe someday I can read the newspapers, maybe even write them. Life is funny like that!" Davide spewed.

"And the reward? Is it worthy of honor?" Esposito asked.

"It could be a million lire, but what does that matter? Only a fool will talk and point a finger. His life will be forfeited an hour after his mouth opens," Davide offered.

"That is true, cugino. Fear is our power in these hills. Fear that we will kill, fear that we will not allow the water to flow onto the farms and gardens, fear that we will kidnap the son of the spacchime mine owners or anyone else with a bundle of lire," Leone announced. Everyone toasted to Leone's soliloquy on fear. Small glasses, filled with vino di casa, the homemade wine made by Davide and his wife, Federica. They took such pride in serving their notorious cousin and his cohorts.

"How long will we keep running from this army without getting what is due us, Anto? Enough time has passed without a message being sent to that fucking Rose," Esposito seethed.

"Beppe, you let your temper get in your way too much. If it was up to you, this package we have, would have been dead weeks ago, and we would have nothing to show for our labor. But, my dear friend, you are right. Enough of this bullshit Rose and his partner Gardner throw at us. So tomorrow, Salvatore and Nicola will go into Lercara and spread the word that we will be soon sending a final letter," Leone pronounced.

"Final? Then I can put this English dog to the knife, Anto?" Esposito blurted.

"Madonna mia, when will you learn to have some patience? Final is final when I say it is final. Until then, this prisoner of war we have is a pile of money. Dead, he is a pile of rotting flesh."

"So, another letter?" Esposito asked. His tone was sarcastic which irked Leone.

Leone glared at his lieutenant and spoke slowly, almost in a whisper.

"This letter will make them sit up and listen to me. I will address the wife. She will be told we will first send her husband's ears in a kerchief. That will be followed by his stubby thumbs, and then, finally, and that's when I mean finally, if we don't have our twenty thousand pounds, his small dick will be sent to her in a nice, wooden box."

Esposito erupted in laughter, as did the others, except for Federica, who blushed red with embarrassment at hearing of the dick in the presence of other men.

"And what use will she have of him without his tool, Anto? She will kill him herself! Anto Leone, you are truly a genius." Esposito again exploded in laughter before offering a toast of one hundred years of life for his padrone.

CHAPTER 12

Maria Salerno, mother of four children, a recently widowed miner's wife, is faced with the most difficult decision of her young life. Her eldest son, Aspanu, who is just about to turn five years old, will be sold to work in desperately unsafe and unhealthy conditions in a sulfur mine to put food on her table for the other three, small children. Maria thought for a second about what her friend Elvira Panepinto had mentioned, but prostituting herself was too degrading to herself, her children, and the memory of her husband. Aspanu, as the eldest male child, had to take on the burden of the family in spite of his tender age.

Maria returned to the small house on Via Cimò after giving her word to the picconieri for Aspanu to begin working on the mines the day after tomorrow.

Now she had to explain to her son what was in store for him. Maria fed the children some soup made with some lamb bones and greens, and a small amount of macaroni with olive oil and garlic. A sprinkle of pecorino cheese, that she traded for a week ago for some eggs her hens had dropped, added to the day's nutrition for her family.

"Aspanu, let the others get into bed. Mama wants to talk with you for a while," Maria whispered. She felt her stomach tighten and a warm flash passed over her entire body. Maria had to hold on tightly to the back of a chair as she felt light headed.

"Of course, Mama. We have important things to discuss," Aspanu stated. He held his head high and pumped his tiny chest out with the pride of now being the man of the family.

The children were all settled after Maria softly sang a lullaby to them. The words were touching and sad. Her voice was hoarse from crying all day. The scene became even more sad for Maria when she noticed her husband's idle flute. It was standing next to the chair where he left it the night before he was swallowed by the mine and disappeared from them forever.

Ebbò, ebbò, ebbò
The baby is sleeping
Under a basil plant,
Everybody is sleeping and you aren't,
If you don't want to sleep
I'm going to tell papà.
Ebbò, ebbò, ebbò
This little baby has fallen asleep.

Maria sang this song in a deep, emotional voice so the children would remember their father. Only Aspanu was old enough to keep some memory of his Papà.

Maria took Aspanu by the hand and led him into the garden at the rear of their home. The aroma of ripe, prickly pears and newly-grown basil filled the tiny backyard with a scent which reminded Maria of her childhood. Now, she was a Mama with enormous problems, but the scent calmed her nerves a bit.

"My son, we must talk about how we continue now that Papà has been taken from us," Maria began.

"Mama, I know I must start to work, and I am ready to do what is needed. Please, your face looks like you are about to cry, but we can't cry all the time, Mama," Aspanu offered.

"My sweet boy. You talk like a man already. You are so strong and sure of yourself. But the work will not be easy. Life will not be easy for you. Aspanu, you will be working in the sulfur mine."

"Just like my Papà!" Aspanu blurted.

"Yes, like Papà. Only, you will come back to me because I will pray hard every day to Santa Barbara so she protects you."

"I am happy to be working to help us. I am not afraid, Mama. Papà was brave everyday as I will be. Don't worry, my Mama."

Maria was dying with sadness inside her body. Looking at his mop of dark hair and big, oval, brown eyes, she wanted to scream at

Jesus for being the criminal, the thief who took away her husband 's life and her son's childhood.

She fought back tears and smiled instead.

"There is good news, Aspanu. You and Carlo will be working together, with the same picconieri, and you will not be separated from each other. His name is Signore Alia, and he is very kind, and he has a baby boy. He has worked in the mines since he was a young boy. He will teach you boys about the mines, and you will listen to his every word."

"So, Carlo and I will be as we were every day. I will talk to Carlo all the time and we will make the work like play. Like a game, Mama."

Maria felt a lump come up from her aching stomach and settle into her throat. She had all to do but grab Aspanu into her bosom and scream at the heavens. Her feelings toward God, and baby Jesus, and Mother Mary and all the saints she had been taught about as a little girl had turned to complete disdain. Maria suddenly recalled the woman on the church of SS Maria Della Neve's steps that morning and the woman's unspeakable bitterness. Maria now understood why that older woman spoke with such disrespect.

Aspanu was acting happy and brave, for his mother's sake. The boy had heard stories of the carusi and what some of the picconieri expected them to do. Not only about the hard work but about the disgusting things those men did to the young boys. He heard about the horrible stink that emanated from the men as well as the sometimes dizzying, foul odor of the sulfur mine. He knew about the finches that were brought down into the mines in their small cages, and how if the birds died with their feet sticking upwards, it was time to run as fast as possible for fresh air. He heard about the long hours and sickening heat and the parasites that ate at the miner's and carusi insides. He heard how his back would be sore every day. Aspanu was indeed afraid in spite of the bravado he displayed to his Mama. The night his Papà died, Aspanu dreamt of his Papà coming home, this time his father was naked, smelling of sulfur and sweat, warning his son to take care of himself below ground and to stay alert at all times.

"Mama, if you like, I can start tomorrow when the sun rises. I'm ready to work for my family!" Aspanu boasted.

"No, not tomorrow, my dear son. Tomorrow we will sing songs and laugh, and make plans for the feast days ahead, and then, after supper, will we cut your hair so you are ready to work the next day. Tomorrow, we will have a celebration, and I will roast a chicken in your honor. In the evening, you will meet Signore Alia and he will give you instructions. I will ask Carlo's mother if she and Carlo can join us for some sweets. Tomorrow is your day, Aspanu!"

Aspanu's stomach went into a spasm from the thought of what he was about to begin. He saw himself, in his mind's-eye, suffocating in the mine as so many others had. The thought of a roast chicken and sweets was not even appealing to him. He thought he would throw it up for the dog and the chickens to eat.

Maria knew all along Aspanu was afraid. She knew he was sending a false bravado for her benefit. Maria's instincts, as a mother, read her son's feelings right through his puffed-up chest and squared-off jaw.

"My little, brave man. This family is fortunate to have you as the eldest son. One day, your brothers and sister will know what you have done for them, and you will forever be a man of respect," Maria beamed, while she stifled an eruption of sobs and tears.

"That's if I live until I'm seven," Aspanu thought.

CHAPTER 13

On the afternoon of the Sunday mass, said for the miners and carusi who lost their lives at the Gardner-Rose sulfur mine in Lercara Friddi, Monsignor Giacomo Paci received word from the Cathedral of the Assumption of Virgin Mary in Palermo his request to visit the Archbishop was accepted.

Paci left the next morning from the train station in Lercara Bassa for the ride to Palermo Centrale station.

The Monsignor was met by two priests who escorted him from the rail station by carriage to the cathedral. Paci had not been to Palermo in seven years when, at that time, the Centrale was under construction. He marveled at the massive, new structure and its classical design. Being in Lercara Friddi for so long made Palermo look enormous, practically overwhelming to the monsignor.

Archbishop Michelangelo Celesia, the Benedictine Monk who was elevated to his position by Pope Pius IX in 1871, met with Paci in his palatial office inside the cathedral grounds. The cathedral itself is a magnificent structure of Norman, Moorish, Gothic, Baroque, and Renaissance construction, attesting with brick and mortar to the history of the conquests of Sicily. The archbishop's office somewhat resembled the apostolic palace in Rome, with gold trim on everything, from the furniture to the tea service.

With nuns and young priests scampering around the archbishop's office, seeing to his every whim, the seventy-nine-year-old Archbishop Celesia resembled an old, Arab Sultan in full sovereignty of his domain. Seeing Celesia in his lush surroundings, it was difficult to believe he was the religious leader of arguably the most impoverished of the twenty Italian regions.

"Your Eminence, I am honored to see you again," Monsignor Paci declared. He kissed the aging Archbishop's ring with deserved reverence.

"Welcome, Monsignor. I was hoping to see you at my birthday celebration, but I know how busy you are tending to your duties in your community."

How could I have been there without an invitation? Paci thought.

"My flock is quite large, Eminence. As you know, Lercara Friddi is often called 'Little Palermo' due to the commerce and swelled population."

"The sulfur mines have brought many to your area, Monsignor Paci. This is why we are disappointed in the contributions that flow from your churches. What are there, seven or eight churches just in your town alone?"

"Yes, Eminence, there are eight. Unfortunately, our faithful are suffering greatly from the lower sulfur demand since the mineral was discovered in the United States. And the high taxes, of course. Many of the mines have closed, and so many souls are not working, those who are working have been experiencing significantly lower wages. Of late, Your Eminence, there is a growing number of our loyal parishioners who are immigrating to the United States and Australia looking to escape the poverty that has befallen us," Paci replied.

"I'm certain you can do better, Monsignor. I will continue to pray for the Holy Ghost to inspire you to find ways to make a better showing," Celesia said.

"Your prayers are always welcome, Your Eminence."

"So, I understand from your letter that you are looking for guidance on a few issues that are pressing to you," the Archbishop offered.

"Eminence, there is clamor among the miners and the field workers and their families regarding the working conditions at the mines and in the agricultural fields. There are also excise tariffs which are strangling the workers. The people are coming to me in hopes that I can intervene on their behalf with the mine owners as well as the land owners. There is a group, the Fasci Siciliani..." Paci's thought was interrupted by the Archbishop.

"Monsignor, these things you speak of are not for the church to be in conflict with. The landlords and mine owners are quite generous to the ministry here in Palermo. Frankly, many of them are not even Catholic, yet they show their respect to this office and to the Holy Father. I must remind you about the wealth and power of the Whitaker, the Rose and Gardner families. It is inconceivable to me that we would interfere with their business especially when they are providing so many needed jobs in Sicily."

"Respectfully, Eminence, young children are being used as indentured servants, slaves if you will excuse the word, to carry sulfur ore to the surface, with little pay and no possibility to live a...."

The archbishop interrupted the monsignor again.

"My dear, Giacomo. You sound like this socialist group of insurrectionists, the Fasci Siciliani you mention. Trust me when I tell you that by next year, that rabble will be jailed and disbanded by government forces. Believe me, Giacomo, I have made my career getting close to the men who control the politics of Italy. I have had several conversations on these troublemakers with Prime Minister Giovanni Giolitti in Rome and our former prime minister, Francesco Crispi, who is staying here in Palermo. However, I believe that Giolitti will soon be out of office. That banking scandal looms large at the moment. My old friend Crispi will likely return as Prime Minister. Incidentally, Crispi is the first, Sicilian-born man to hold that esteemed office. He understands full well the poverty of the south. It seems that our own government respects the investment these honorable families have made to Sicily. I expect that you show that same respect."

"Eminence, I respect the fact that these foreigners have taken their business acumen and investment to Lercara Friddi and other towns within our Island. I am simply seeking some relief for these impoverished faithful, who are begging for Holy Mother Church to intercede on their behalf for better working conditions and better pay," Paci implored.

"The Holy See, his Holiness Pope Leo the thirteenth, who himself elevated me to my position, would be with rue to interfere with establishments who are doing their part in feeding the masses of the poor in our communities. Certainly, you are not here to advocate the church or the government set aside alms for these souls? We live in terrible times, Monsignor, when our role is to propagate the faith and lead souls to Christ. Nowhere is it the responsibility of Holy Mother Church to use our influence or our pulpits to condemn generous men and criticize how they run their business affairs."

"I fully understand, Your Eminence. I thank you for your wisdom and guidance," Paci blurted. What he was thinking was the polar opposite.

"Anything else, my son? If not, I would be pleased to show you around the gardens. Oh...I have a special evening planned for us. After dinner, we will be going to the Politeama Garibaldi to enjoy a concert conducted by Arturo Toscanini. And tomorrow night, I trust you will enjoy dinner with me and my friend Francesco Crispi at his residence. When you taste what his chefs prepare for our dinner, you will truly feel you have died and gone to heaven.

"I am honored, Your Eminence," Paci replied.

I have sold myself like any politician, Paci thought.

CHAPTER 14

Maria woke early, before sunlight, with a tightness in her belly that reminded her of the beginning of childbirth. It promised to be a warm day in Lercara Friddi, and the hoped-for rain would not come. The drought had become a problem, and water for the plants was scarce. She looked at each of her four children, asleep in the same bed, knowing that tomorrow Aspanu would be waking to his first day as a carusi.

The young widow was desperately unhappy with her decision to take money for Aspanu's hard labor, for his childhood, and possibly for life itself. Maria was sentencing her eldest child to imprisonment in the sulfur mines so the rest of the family didn't starve, simply because he was next in line to his father.

And what would be when her next son became of age to be a carusu? And her baby son just a few years from now. *Will I lose them all to the mines like I lost my husband?* Maria thought.

The young widow knelt before the small altar to Santa Barbara and Our Lady and began to pray for help and hope. While she tried to pray, Maria remembered the voices of the women on the steps of the church and how they had become embittered and sacrilegious. Her prayers were interloped by her thoughts. Maria began to think her prayers were futile and she was wasting her time being devoted to plaster and wood figures. Tears began to run down her dark, thin cheeks. Unexpectedly, Maria felt something touch her shoulder. She looked down to see Aspanu's little hand.

"Buongiorno, Mama!"

"Ah, Aspanu, buongiorno."

"Today is a beautiful day, Mama. And every day will be beautiful, no matter what if we are all together, me, you, my two baby brothers, and my baby sister," Aspanu decreed.

"My sweet boy. You are so much like your Papà."

"And every day we will begin by saying 'it's a beautiful day' even if it's raining, snowing, or so hot the ground hurts our feet."

"We will, Aspanu. I will teach the children, and we will say a small prayer to Santa Barbara for you every day."

"So, today, I must gather wood for your stove, work in the garden to pull the weeds, fix the fence in the garden, and bring water from the well. Then later, I will have my haircut," Aspanu said quickly.

"I wanted today to be a day of holding hands and singing and playing games. I thought you and Carlo would have the roasted chicken together. His mother will bring some things from her garden and some sweets, and we...."

"Mama, there is no time to do little boy things. I still have my chores. Tomorrow I go to work and my chores will meet me after I return. If I am to be a man, I must be a man. Your little boys are asleep in that bed."

Maria was speechless. Here, this almost five-year-old boy had become the head of the family overnight.

"But Mama, your idea for a roasted chicken and sweets is excellent," Aspanu announced. Mother and son laughed aloud, almost awakening the smaller children.

◊◊◊

Elvira came to the Salerno house with Carlo and her other children before dusk for the roast chicken dinner. Carlo grabbed Aspanu's newly-shorn head, Aspanu doing the same to his friend.

"Our heads look like melons, Carlo. I think my melon is bigger."

"But my melon looks more like an eggplant," Carlo laughed. Aspanu agreed.

The boys laughed and faked a fistfight while their mothers worked to make the meal for both families of the new carusi. There likely would be no meal again like this until Christmas, and there was no guarantee another chicken would be available this coming winter.

The plump chicken's neck was pulled and broken and plucked the night before. Maria was taught the chicken tasted better when it rested for a day after its neck was broken.

Maria made a stuffing of stale, homemade bread with the liver and heart and gizzards of the chicken, some herbs from the garden, dark, fat raisins, and a few chestnuts. Elvira brought string beans made in olive oil and garlic with toasted almonds on top with a sprinkling of pecorino cheese. Every part of the meal came from her tiny garden and trees. She also had some cold peas and macaroni she made earlier in the day which they would heat on the stove. Milk from both family goats would be served in small cups with an admonition to sip, not drink.

Elvira's "sweets" were more like pastries. They were her specialty. She called them pantofole. An elongated cookie that was stuffed with almond filling and dried fruit pieces, they resembled slippers which had a sugar glaze on top.

As the meal was served, the eyes of the children were as big as the biggest, blackest olives ever seen. But first a few prayers to Our Lady of Constantinople and Santa Barbara. Carlo and Aspanu tried to help their little brothers and sisters to bless themselves. Aspanu looked at Carlo and laughed at his head again. Carlo returned the favor.

The meal lasted for a long while, with singing and laughing, yet everyone was having a very unusual and uncomfortable feeling; their bellies were full for the first time in a very long time.

◊◊◊

It was now getting dark, so Maria put on a pot of coffee for her and Elvira, who poured the goats milk for the children and served her delicious slippers. The end of the evening was here.

As if by signal, when the last slipper was eaten and the crumbs were being picked up by little fingers from the table, there was a knock on the door.

Maria and Elvira felt their hearts sink into their stomachs. Reality was on the other side of the door.

It was Signore Alia—coming to pay the soccorso di morti to buy Aspanu and Carlo.

Tomorrow morning would be the end of innocence for these two boys.

CHAPTER 15

The letter from Antonino Leone was stuck to the front door at Villa Lisetta with a six-inch black and silver stiletto.

"Dear Signora Rose, The knife that has pierced this letter has a sister. I will use her to carve the ears off your husband, and they will be sent to you. Then his thumbs will follow.

I accept your offer of five thousand pounds. A bargain for your husband's life. You will bring the pounds yourself to the train station in Lercara Bassa in a box that will be made obvious. Should there be any carabinieri or soldiers nearby, you will find your husband's dead body with his manhood removed. You have two days to bring my money. Come alone, after dark. Leone."

Elizabeth Gardner-Rose, her husband's parents, and Comandante Greco sat in the Rose study. Tea and cookies were served. The bandit's letter was placed on the large, dark, mahogany desk by Greco when he was finished reading.

"Signora Rose, I suggest you do exactly what Leone is demanding. It has been twenty days since your husband has been taken. I believe that Mr. Forester will be murdered if you don't comply," Comandante Greco assured her.

"I agree. The money is here and ready to be delivered. I will bring it myself. I will go by carriage and lantern to the station," Elizabeth proclaimed. The young woman's stomach flipped at the thought of going in the dark alone.

"And what is stopping these arch criminals from way laying you, taking the money and leaving you for dead?" Mr. Rose asked.

Elizabeth stood from the tufted, winged chair in which she sat and placed her hands on her hips in defiance. She spoke with command in her voice, "Fear is what is stopping them, Father! I believe Leone to be a coward among many other despicable things, but he is not stupid. He knows he is hunted and will continue to be hunted after kidnapping John. The word that got to him about my family being rebels in our war of independence hit a nerve. Now, I will take the funds to the station, tomorrow night, and that will be the end of this nightmare."

"And if they murder my son and leave him in a cave somewhere in these hills anyway?"

"Then Father, that would be his destiny. I do not believe Leone will do that. He will kidnap again. If he kills my husband after I have paid, he will never get another penny for his next kidnapping victims. He will take this money and run, and we will have John back, in one piece," Elizabeth answered.

Greco laid his tea cup down on a dark, inlaid cherry wood table and cleared his throat.

"I agree with Signora Gardner-Rose, totally. Leone wants this to end. He knows that five thousand pounds can get him and his cohorts out of Sicily for the time being. Perhaps Malta, Tunisia, somewhere where he can hide for a while. Leone will return John Forester soon after the money is received. I suggest we don't try to capture anyone who comes for the funds. Certainly, it will not be Leone himself. Most likely, Esposito or another confederate. If we make a move to apprehend someone at that station, John Forester will no doubt be summarily executed," Greco declared.

"Comandante, you seem to know how to communicate with Leone. Leone does indeed have eyes and ears everywhere. Get word to him that I will be at Lercara Bassa station at eight tomorrow evening," Elizabeth stated.

"Yes, Signora. I think this is the right way to bring this to a reasonable conclusion," Greco uttered.

◊◊◊

On the outskirts of Marineo, Leone and his crew had grown comfortable being guests of the bandit's cousin Federica and her Davide. There was something about Davide that Giuseppe Esposito did not trust. He couldn't quite put his feelings into words but that didn't prevent him from saying something to Leone.

The two men walked in the moon, smoking short cigars, the night the final letter was sent to Elizabeth Rose. Their stomachs were full from another delicious, rustic meal prepared by Federica and Davide.

"Anto, I don't like his eyes...your cousin's husband. There is no trust in that man. His eyes dart too much for me," Esposito said.

"Ah, Beppe! You are jealous. I see the way you look at Feddy. It's been too long since you've been with a woman."

"Perhaps, but he reminds me of a ferret. That is like a rat, no? Anyway, when this is over I will go into Palermo and get myself fixed up with a woman I know there. Take in an opera or a musical...have fun and enjoy myself for once."

"Are you horny or just stupid? Everyone in Sicily is looking for us. We will go into hiding for a while and return with something that will make minstrels sing for a thousand years," Leone declared.

"When I dress up nicely, I look like a banker. I can sit in front of the Pope and they will never know who I am," Esposito laughed.

"You will spend time figuring out our escape plans. Then we will discuss your return to the Politeama Garibaldi with your latest concubine."

The men returned to the house, removed John Forester Rose from his makeshift cell, and removed his bindings. It was time Leone cleared his conscience in case the money never came.

"I have to say, Signore Rose. We kept you well-fed, especially the past few days. Actually, we may have fattened you up a bit with all the pasta, bread, and wine you've consumed. Except for your beard, your young wife will be happy about your condition," Leone said.

"I have lost track of the time. How long have you held me?"

"Twenty-one days tomorrow. I must be frank. If I were you, I would be insulted that my father and my wife were so cheap and would allow us to kill you like a dog. I don't have money, so I guess I have no idea how I'd behave if I were rich."

"It has nothing to do with money, sir!" John exclaimed.

"Then what? Money makes the work go-round, Signore. It's always about money...everything on earth is about money," Leone shouted. The bandit was frustrated with the Englishman's arrogance.

"My family has drawn a line in the sand. They will not allow us, as a family, to be extorted."

"That's how much you know, curnutu. Your pretty wife wanted to bargain for your life. She offered a third of what I demanded. I accepted her offer. I have other people to rob, people richer than you and your arrogant family." Leone was standing over the seated John Forester Rose and screaming at him. Once or twice, Leone had an urge to bash the young Englishman's face in.

"I would have advised her not to have negotiated with the likes of you, Leone. My ancestors went into battle and let their fate be as it may. I have no fear of dying," John Forester uttered. The opposite was true, the young man was bluffing all the way.

"We shall see my friend. Tomorrow night, we await your wife to bring us our just rewards. If she reneges, or tries to have our man arrested, my friend here, Signore Giuseppe Esposito, as is his want, will carve you up like an Easter lamb, and the pigs will devour your innards. Maybe even while you watch. And that, Signore Rose, will be your wife's doing," Leone stated. He was calmer now. His conscience was scrubbed clean in his own mind.

CHAPTER 16

Maria woke her son at five in the morning. Aspanu hardly slept knowing today was his first day of work at the Gardner-Rose mine. Maria did not sleep at all. How could she?

The house was quiet, save for the sleepy, heavy breathing from the other children who were huddled in the large bed. Aspanu had a strange sensation in his stomach, one he never had before.

"Mama, my stomach has twitching inside. Maybe I ate too much last night or the slippers are kicking the chicken. Did Papà ever have this twitching?" Aspanu giggled.

"My beautiful son, you are just excited to start your job. This will pass once you begin working. I didn't know Papà when he started working in the mines as a carusu, and he never told me if he had them, but I'm certain he did."

Maria waved Aspanu to the table. Candles on the table and in front of the statues of Our Lady and Santa Barbara cast eerie shadows around the room.

"I have some bread with some green olives and some milk that I put aside for you. Eat slowly. Soon Carlo will meet you on the corner and you will walk together to the mines. Please obey Signore Alia, he will teach you what you need to do for your job."

"Signore Alia seems to be a nice man. He is quiet like Papà was. He told Carlo and me that ours is a very important job. Without us, they cannot bring the sulfur to the surface," Aspanu bragged.

"Yes, it is very important," Maria whispered choking back a cry.

"Signore Alia said every basket of sulfur is counted at the surface, and we are to bring what we carry to the oven. I know Carlo and I will make the daily tally that Signore Alia talked about before all the other carusi," Aspanu blurted. He dunked the stale bread into the milk to soften it. When he bit into the bread, the milk ran down his throat with a refreshing feeling. The butterflies in his stomach continued.

Aspanu finished his meager breakfast quickly, making sure he ate every crumb of bread that fell on his plate.

"Aspanu, soon you must leave, but before you do, I think we need to kneel to Our Lady and Santa Barbara and say a short prayer and of course a Hail Mary," Maria whispered.

"Sure, Mama, can you help with the prayers? I always forget the words of the Hail Mary prayer."

Maria hugged her son as he sat in the chair. It was always his father's chair at the head of the table. It was now Aspanu's chair.

Aspanu brushed away his mother's gushy kisses but held onto her as tightly as she hugged him. After a long pause, the mother and son knelt before the tiny shrine and blessed themselves. Maria led the Hail Mary and Aspanu followed. His prayer was flawless. Then a short prayer to Santa Barbara to protect the new carusu and bring him home safely was implored by Maria.

They blessed themselves to finish the prayer when a cock crowed a few houses down.

"Now I'm off to work! Where is my bag and my cap?" Aspanu demanded. His stomach did a full flip in spite of his outward bravado.

"Aspanu, here is your cap. Inside the bag is a tin cup for you to drink water from. Drink whenever you are able, my son. In the bag, there is a cube of sugar and an apple if you need something to hold you over." Maria barely got the words out. This is the moment she was dreading since she decided to take the soccorso di morti from Domenico Alia.

"Goodbye, Mama. Please kiss my brothers and baby sister when they wake. I will be home tonight." Aspanu turned, and he was out of the door in a flash. Maria bit her trembling right hand so hard she drew blood.

It was still dark outside, but the sun was making its way over the horizon. Some of the larger houses on Via Cimò were still casting shadows giving a melodramatic start to the day. The cobblestoned streets had a light sheen of dew. A neighbor's cat ran past Aspanu while carrying a small mouse in its mouth. The boy was happy for the cat and sad for the mouse. "But this is how life goes," Aspanu thought.

Here came Carlo, with his shoulder bag and cap just like Aspanu. Both barefoot, they felt the coolness of the cobblestones as they walked toward each other.

"Buongiorno, pisano," Carlo said.

"It's a beautiful day," Aspanu replied.

"We are off to be the men of our families. Did you sleep well?" Carlo inquired.

"Like a baby!" Aspanu fibbed.

"Me, too. My Mama had to shake a few times to wake me," Carlo lied.

Carlo continued, "I must tell, I think I ate too much last night. My stomach has a funny feeling. Like a bird is inside trying to escape."

"I feel the same. Mama said it will pass once we start to work. I think I ate too much too, Carlo."

"My Mama was almost crying."

"Mine, too. They will get used to us working," Aspanu uttered.

The two carusi waked with their chests out, with heads held high for a bit more than a mile to the sulfur yard. As they walked, they saw other carusi, walking with their heads down and their shoulders slumped. Miners came out of their homes or from around the street corners, almost all of them smoking a small, dark, twisted cigar, or a pipe, heading in the same direction toward the mine.

As the boys entered the Gardner-Rose property, they could smell the acrid aroma of sulfur, an odor they were used to since birth. It wasn't at all an unpleasant smell to them, but a smell nonetheless. They were quickly enveloped with other carusi and picconieri, all walking in silence as the sun began to rise quickly over the horizon, bringing light and a comfortable warmth to the morning.

The boys saw Domenico Alia, standing tall with a pick axe over his shoulder. He was looking around the entrance to the mine area when he spotted Aspanu and Carlo. He smiled broadly at his new property as a shrill whistle sounded the beginning of the work day. Both boys touched their stomachs to perhaps in some way soothe their nerves.

They were now officially carusi.

CHAPTER 17

Domenico Alia was ready to start a day's work with his new carusi. Picconieri, carusi, traders, carters, merchandisers, and craftsmen hurried in different directions around the mine, adding to the frenetic fever the owners established for their unbridled greed.

"There are a few things I need to tell you as we go down into the mine. First of all, take off your shoulder bags and leave them over there near the pile of stones. Don't worry, this is not the mine where your fathers were lost. That will be closed for a long time. Now, always remember my whistle and come to me as soon as you hear it," Domenico Alia instructed. The picconieri pursed his lips and let out a whistle that sounded like a wounded bird. It was his signature signal the two boys could not afford to mistake or duplicate. Alia's voice sounded as if his throat was hurting him. He coughed often and spit after every cough.

"See that man, the dark one who looks like a small bull? He is the gabbelloto, everyone's boss. Signore Giuseppe Modica, and he is a real animal. Make sure when you see him, you are moving as quickly as you can, or his hoof will be in your ass. If he thinks you are taking advantage of the clock, it will be a bad day for you and for me. Modica loves to levy fines. He calls them a tax. Bastard! Luckily, he is the boss of the entire mine, so we don't see him much and never below ground. Understand?" Alia asked.

"Yes signore," Aspanu and Carlo replied. Their voices both quivered from nerves. Their little stomachs were ready to spew the small breakfasts they ate.

"Here is the vucca, the entrance of the mine. Pay attention to the dirt and stone steps. They cannot be trusted. These steps are sometimes slippery, they are not straight, and they often crumble. You don't want to carry a load up all the way and drop half of it as you come up. After a while, you will know these steps like you know your own feet. Look at the top of the vucca, will you?"

Over the mine's entrance was a pair of huge bull's horns with some writing underneath. Aspanu and Carlo looked up, not knowing how to read the words.

"It says, 'These horns will ward off the evil eye for all who enter,' They protect us... except when they don't."

"They didn't protect my Papà so good," Carlo thought.

Alia pointed down to some things that rested on the side of the mine opening.

"Each of you, pick up a basket. I will show you the proper way to carry them on your shoulder." The baskets were woven from green and brown pieces of olive trees. They were smooth to the touch.

"Now, you take the basket in your right hand, from the top, using your left hand to balance. Now lift it onto your left shoulder. Your head should be ahead of the basket at all times," Alia instructed.

Both carusi lifted their basket and did exactly as they were told. Both of their knees wobbled, not from the lightweight of the carrier, but from nerves.

"Now put them down into your right hand for a moment. Each of you, take a lantern in your left hand. This is the only light that we have down in the shafts. A flame will make the sulfur gas explode and kill everyone, but these lamps are made special, so don't worry. I will explain how they work another time. Right now, we have to start working on our daily load."

"Any questions?" Alia asked. He coughed up some phlegm and spit out a wad in front of him.

Aspanu and Carlo followed the spit with their eyes. They never saw anything so heavy come out of a man's mouth.

"Hey, wake up! Any questions?"

"No, signore," they answered in tandem.

"In this wooden cage, is a bird called a goldfinch. I've had this one for almost a year. His name is Beppe. I feed him, give him water, and let him stay with other finches at night when we leave. This way, they make baby finches for us to use. If he falls to the bottom of the cage and his toes point up, it means he has died from sulfur gas. If you see that, make your way to the surface as fast as your feet will take you."

"Now we go, but wait, one more thing. When you bring your baskets to the surface, look...see over there? That is where you will bring the sulfur, into the calcaroni. That is where the ore is melted into a liquid and then hardened again and made ready for shipment. We are judged and paid by our volume of sulfur we produce from inside the mine. So, no dilly dallying up here on the surface. Dump the load, breathe the fresh air in deeply and return to where I am immediately."

"Ready? Now we enter the mine and go to the level where we will be pulling the sulfur from the walls. Stay close behind me all the way down," Alia pronounced.

Alia bounded into the mine with Aspanu and Carlo on his heels. Carlo slipped on the second step, but Aspanu held him up and steadied his friend. The walls of the mine shaft were gray and then became dark as the morning light only snuck in for a few yards. The lamps the two carusi carried emitted a flat, greyish light which gave them ten yards of light at best.

The shaft was tight. Just enough for Alia to fit if he lowered his head a bit. Aspanu and Carlo, at almost five years old, had plenty of room to maneuver.

As they moved down the shaft, the acrid odor of sulfur filled their nostrils and throats, both boys momentarily remembering the smell of their late fathers. The lower into the mine they went, the less fresh air there was to breathe, and the warmer it became. Beads of perspiration had already begun to form on the carusi's foreheads. Both boys could feel drops of sweat running down their backs and soaking through their shirts.

They arrived at the first landing after about five minutes in the mine shaft. The gray walls were scratched by picks until there was no more yellow ore in the rocks to be seen.

Alia stopped short and farted.

"Two bad for you two. My wife made me a plate of beans for my supper last night. I'll be tooting all day. I hope Beppe doesn't die from my gas," Alia joked. He laughed heartily at his own joke, the laugh echoing in the open space of the first level.

Aspanu was standing directly behind his picconiere and took the brunt of it. He gagged from the stink, just enough to spit up enough sputum to leave an acidic film in his mouth and throat.

"The further we go down, the hotter it gets. Right now, this early in the morning, it's not so bad. By noon, one o'clock it will be one hundred and sixteen degrees where we are working. So, leave your clothes here, all of them. Before you go outside with your load, at least tie your shorts to cover your balls and ass," Alia ordered. He also stripped totally, leaving his clothing in a pile with the carusi.

"Amuninni...let's go. I'm behind schedule already," Alia growled.

Aspanu was embarrassed to be naked in front of his friend Carlo and Alia and also other carusi and picconieri who were already filling their baskets. He held the olive tree basket in front of his private parts, nearly dropping the lamp.

Alia turned to see what the noise was and quickly corrected Aspanu. "Hold the basket in one hand on one side and the lamp on the other side by its handle."

Carlo and Aspanu got a glimpse of Alia's manhood and quickly looked away. They were as shocked as they were embarrassed.

A picconieri was working with three carusi on the second landing. His name was Vincenzo Dolce, and his reputation among the carusi was that of a brutal man. Dolce's boys were older than Aspanu and Carlo. Around twelve or thirteen years old, also naked as the day they were born except for their caps over their nearly bald heads. They already had hair under their arms and around their balls. Two of the carusi had the beginnings of a slight moustache that their sweat and dust from the picking exenterated.

"Oh, Domenico, I see today you are breaking in virgins. Leave them by me, and I'll show them the ropes," the miner said. He thrust his hips in and out in a sexual gesture. He whistled at Aspanu and Carlo.

"Dolce, you are a curnutu. These are my boys, so keep your filthy hands from them or I'll bury my pick into your back. Understood?" Alia countered.

"Very touchy, I see. When they fall down on their faces I'll buy them from you for half of what you paid," Dolce blurted loudly, his voice echoing off the gray walls.

"Up your ass, cafone. You are a disgrace." Alia replied. He kept walking down the shaft, and his boys followed quickly behind.

"Okay, here we are. This will be your station until these walls are finished with sulfur ore. It should take us about two weeks here...maybe more. Now, as I pick at the walls, you both take the rocks and fill your baskets as high as you can."

Alia took the pick axe from his shoulder, and dropped the heavy end to the floor. The axe handle rested on his muscular thigh. The picconieri dribbled a gob of spit into his hands and rubbed them together. He lifted the axe and slammed it into the wall of stone. On his second hit, chunks of stone fell to the ground. Aspanu and Carlo scampered for the sulfur-laced rocks and began to fill their baskets with enthusiasm.

CHAPTER 18

Late in the day, Aspanu and Carlo started their life as carusi and would begin paying back the soccorso di morti Domenico Alia, Monsignor Giacomo Paci returned from seeing the Archbishop in Palermo.

Paci had an empty feeling on the train ride back to Lercara Bassa. By the time he took the short carriage ride to Lercara Friddi, the monsignor was literally in tears. The vacant sense of defeat and failure erupted in the monsignor's spirit, just after the lavish dinner he and his ecclesiastical superior had with the former, and likely soon to be the next prime minister of Italy, Francesco Crispi. Paci could see how Crispi and the Archbishop played each other like a game of chess.

There was nothing Paci could do for the desperate mine workers, the wretched carusi, or the exploited farm workers in his parish or the other churches in the hill towns of western Sicily. At least not if he wanted to stay in his position of archpriest of Lercara Friddi and not find himself transferred to a grass hut in Ethiopia.

Monsignor Paci and the most estimable person in Lercara had a dinner appointment that was scheduled weeks before, in the person of Doctor Alfonso Giordano. Paci was tired and a bit depressed from his experiences in Palermo. At first, he considered cancelling dinner, but then thought seeing Giordano might lighten his somber mood. They met at the rectory of Santa Maria Della Neve.

"My dear doctor, you are looking quite well. Thank you for having dinner with me tonight," Paci offered. The dining room of the rectory was simple, yet elegant. A long, cherry wood table with a locally hand-woven, lace tablecloth, under an ornate, Capodimonte porcelain, chandelier, was in the center of the room. The chandelier was installed in 1750 as a gift from a wealthy landlord, twenty years after the church was constructed. The landlord had a latifundia, from a Latin word for a large parcel of land that went back to Roman times. Sharecroppers, or mitateri, were basically slaves for the landlord.

Eight, high-backed, carved, cherry wood chairs were placed around the table. On one wall of the dining room, an impressively large oil painting of Pope Leo XIII, the sitting Pontiff, was lit by two candle sconces on either side. The four-foot, wooden crucifix on the adjacent wall had votive candles beneath it, casting a macabre shadow on the dead Christ. A wooden statue of Our Lady, adorned with a crown of fresh flowers, rested on a side buffet table, also illuminated by blessed candles.

Two, elderly, widowed women, dressed in black, floor-length dresses and black lace head covers, served the homemade food and local wine.

"I am delighted to join you, Monsignor. I must have seen half this town in my office today. There is a stomach virus plaguing our Lercara as of late. Nothing serious, thank God," Giordano replied.

"May the good Lord protect us from another outbreak of cholera as we had a few years ago. We lost so many souls. May they all rest in peace," Paci commented.

The women moved slowly around the table, serving the first course of soup with escarole and meatballs. They sprinkled pecorino cheese on the piping hot dish.

"Monsignor, I wanted to visit and talk about mundane things tonight, such as your short trip to Palermo or the weather, but I have things pressing on my mind," Giordano said.

"Tell me, doctor. Is it a confession?"

"No…no, this is not about me and my salvation. I am concerned about the illnesses that I'm seeing among the mine workers. Especially the carusi. You see, the sanitary conditions, especially with toilet conditions in the mines, are worse than ever. Let me explain the worst I'm seeing. I will try in non-medical terms. Ancylostomiasis… let us call it hookworm or miners anemia for our discussion. It's a parasite that enters from wounds on the feet, which enter the lungs, then to the windpipe, and then to the intestines. The parasites work their way into the intestines where they take blood from the walls of the organ. This gives severe iron deficiency. You may also see snake like markings on the skin. This is the parasite that is caught under the skin. Left untreated, after some time, the disease is fatal. We now have some elementary cure methods.   At the worst, a blood transfusion is indicated, but proper diet, some pharmaceuticals, and supplements can defeat this miner's anemia."

"Quite sad," Paci responded.

"Indeed. Here is where I need some assistance from you, Monsignor. My communication with the mine owners have fallen on deaf ears. I have tried many times without results. Bad enough the condition of the mines and the work the children are forced to do have created numerous other serious ailments. Rickets, irreversible pulmonary and ocular diseases, not to mention long-term skeletal dysfunction and deformities around the shoulders. The miners' anemia and pulmonary and eye issues also affect the mature miners as well. I need to change what is going on at the mines to prevent the spread of this disease. A word from you, and I can meet with the mine owners to solve these issues, or at the very least, mitigate them," Giordano proclaimed.

One women cleared away the empty soup bowls and the other served the second dish. A brusciuluni di cutini, a pig skin wrapped with a stuffing of herbs, raisins, and pinoli nuts, served on a bed of freshly made linguine in a red sauce.

"I hope you like this dish, Doctor. My mother made this for us every Sunday for dinner. It is among my favorite things to eat. Perhaps it is too rich for me, but life is about taking small enjoyments whenever possible. After all, if I cut back on my luxuries at the table, perhaps I will live an extra fifteen minutes," Paci pronounced. The monsignor snickered at his own joke.

Doctor Giordano couldn't care less. He wanted to focus on the serious health issues in the community.

"I'm sure it's delicious. Now then, I have had many letters to and from the French microbiologist Louis Pasteur. We have become quite friendly. He has taken a keen interest in the parasite that is plaguing our miners. He agrees that proper sanitation is the key to defeating this disease. He is also working on additional cures with my information. This well-known scientist has been working tirelessly to find a solution. Unfortunately, Professor Pasteur is up in age. He suffered a stroke some years ago, and Pasteur is not very well at the moment. I don't know how long he will be around to help," Gambino proffered.

"I see. One moment, Doctor. Dorotea, please serve some more wine to us. It seems my glass has a small hole in it," Paci joked. His dinner companion didn't find the timing of the humor to be appropriate.

Monsignor Paci continued.

"Alfonso, my friend. There is not much that I can do to help you. Any position that my office takes can be looked upon as interference into the business of the mine owners. I have been instructed by the Archbishop to guard against any intrusion into the commerce of the mines, or the farms for that matter. I am to use my pulpit to preach the word of God, so I'm afraid that there is nothing I can do for you in this regard," Paci stated. The monsignor looked down into his pork rolatene in embarrassed despair.

Doctor Giordano was nonplussed. He paused and felt a heat rising up his neck and into his face.

"Monsignor Paci, I am a scientist. I am well aware of the wide gap between religion and science. But this issue transcends the two. This issue is about human lives that can get some modicum of relief in the living hell of the mines here and all over Sicily. I came to you as the shepherd of your flock. Surely you can empathize with…"

Paci interrupted the doctors thought.

"My soul aches for the abject poverty that I see on a daily basis, Alfonso. The pain and the horror is sometimes too much to take. I am ill over the fact that my hands have been tied behind my back. My orders come from the Archbishop, and his orders come from the Vatican. Please do not press our friendship. I simply cannot help."

CHAPTER 19

Carlo and Aspanu filled their baskets with the rocks lying at the feet of their picconieri, Alia. They lifted the carriers over their shoulders as they had been instructed. The knees of both the soon-to-be-five-year-olds slightly buckled under the nearly seventy-pounds of stones.

Aspanu looked at his friend with a worried yet supportive look. They could do it, said Aspanu's eyes. His body told him otherwise.

With their enthusiasm, both carusi moved quickly up the mine shaft, trying not to pay attention to the remarks and whistles of the picconieri with whom Alia already had words, on their way down into the mine. As they moved upward, the weight of the earth seemed to get heavier. The boys slowed down only because of other carusi who were moving slowly ahead of them.

"Oh, baby boys, you better learn to pace yourself, otherwise your strength will be gone before midday," an older carusu who was ahead of them warned.

"Thank you, but Signore Alia has warned us to work quickly. Tell me, what are those marks on the outside of your thighs from?" Carlo inquired.

"You will soon feel that pain, little one. Yesterday, I was moving slowly, so my picconiere pressed the hot lantern against me after he smacked my head. It happens usually at the end of the day if the man is in a bad mood or he knows his count is low. Trust me, a steady pace is better for you," the older boy replied.

Carlo turned to look at Aspanu, nearly dropping his load of sulfur rock from his basket. His face had a momentary look of terror thinking they would be branded from the lamp. Laying the baskets down slowly, Carlo and Aspanu found their shorts and wrapped them around their bottoms in what looked like a diaper.

As they approached the opening of the mine, they could hear the noises from the surface, smell the molten sulfur from the calcaroni, and see the light of day. The sun had come up bright and hot.

Once on the surface, the semi-fresh air was a relief to their lungs and both of the new carusi filled themselves with the refreshing air.

"Madonna mia, that was a rough trip," Carlo stated. The two friends began walking toward the oven.

"We will get used to it, Carlo. Everything gets easy after a while," Aspanu guessed.

"This is no game, my friend. That boy's legs are pretty scarred by that lamp. Do you think Signore Alia will burn us like that?"

"That picconiere is a strunzu. A real bad man. I think Signore Alia is nicer than him."

Suddenly, a booming voice came from behind them.

"Less talk and more work, you skinny bastards. Let your legs move and your lips stay quiet," Signore Modica hollered. He carried a rubber hose he smashed into his hand making a sickening thump. "If you want to taste this on your ass, just keep talking like two old ladies doing their wash."

The boys moved quickly toward the calcaroni without a sound.

Dozens of carusi hauled their loads onto a metal bin which would feed into the oven. Every miner had their own bin.

When it was Carlo and Aspanu's turn, the boys both saw a young girl who they stared at in awe.

It was Nina Miceli. She was a bit older than the boys and a real beauty. Her huge, hazel eyes kept their attention to the antediluvian scale as she marked a paper which rested on a piece of wood in her hands. Everyone's weight of stone was taken. This is how the picconieri were judged and paid.

Nina's chestnut-brown hair was pulled back into a tight bun, her cap on top, covering her brow. She wore a tattered, plaid, work shirt and thick, work pants, with dark brown, well-worn boots. One boot had heavy twine wrapped around it to hold the worn sole together. Nina never looked up at the carusi. She was there to do her job.

Carlo, ever the daredevil, always the one who would take the risk at things, looked around for Signore Modica. Not seeing him anywhere, Carlo spoke to Nina. He just had to get her attention.

"This is our first day of work, signorina."

Nina looked up quickly and looked back at the old scale.

"Keep quiet, idiot. What does she care who we are and what we are doing?" Aspanu blurted.

"Okay, I just wanted her to see us, is all," Carlo whispered.

"I don't want that rubber thing on my ass or anywhere else. Just stay quiet, we can talk a bit in the shaft."

After dumping the material, the boys turned on their heels and headed back quickly to the vucca and another heavy load.

CHAPTER 20

Aspanu and Carlo made twenty trips up and down the grottacalda, the hot cave, with its gray walls, stinking from every human smell imaginable.

As the day progressed and the sun grew hotter, the picconieri gave off an animal-like body odor which was an affront to the human sense of smell. The aroma from Signore Alia initiated gagging to the two new carusi. The overwhelming foul smell of urine and feces filled the mine. The toilets were on two levels of the mine near the main vent of the mineshaft to lessen the stink, but it was still worse than any animal barn in town. The temperature hit one hundred and sixteen degrees, and the smell from the miner's asses was enough to turn the strongest of stomachs. As the heat rose, so did the foul mood of the picconieri, some of them swearing at the saints and the criminal Jesus Christ. Nothing was left sacred underground. Sporadic screams of the carusi could be heard after they were whipped or smashed for any mistake or perceived slow work by their ill-tempered masters.

At one o'clock in the afternoon, a break was allowed for forty-five minutes. If a picconiere knew his weight count was low, he would call for his boys to return quickly. The carusi, all half-spent, huddled around a cistern of tepid water in an attempt to hydrate themselves. Most of the carusi, especially the ones from the foundling homes, used a communal drinking ladle from which they drank, and poured water over their smoldering heads. Aspanu and Carlo had their own tin cups. The older carusi thought nothing of snatching the little boys' cups from their hands and drinking from them, before they dropped the vessels into the gray muddy earth around the cistern.

The two, new boys were covered in the sulfur ash from head to toe. Both Aspanu and Carlo went to their shoulder bags to take out their meager lunch. Carlo had a small piece of bread, a square of goat cheese, and some green olives. Aspanu had a small apple and a cube of sugar. Instinctively, they hid their food down by their sides not to have the small bit of nourishment swiped from them. Carlo found a small green spider on his bread but shooed it off without worrying about the insect's contamination.

One hundred paces behind the oven was a lone, old and dying, oak tree offering a bit of shade which dozens of carusi laid under for a quick respite. The smell of sweat from the carusi was not very appealing, especially when it was combined with the sulfur smell from the calcaroni, and the sharp smell of old urine around the tree. The boys ate, nonetheless. Aspanu and Carlo ate quickly, the food barely touching their taste buds for fear of the older carusi, some eyeing their small rations, and because they were starving from the enormously hard labor.

"This sun feels good and bad at the same time," Carlo said to Aspanu.

"How do you mean, good and bad?"

"Simple! It feels bad because it can burn your skin, and good because it's not as hot as inside the mine."

"I know, I can hardly breathe down there. Signore Alia must be used to it. He keeps chipping at the walls, over and over. By the time we get back down to him after we dump the load, his pile of stones gets bigger and bigger."

"I don't know which is worse, the smell or the heat...I think maybe the smell," Carlo blurted.

"The thing I like is seeing that girl when we reach the calcaroni. She reminds me of my baby sister somehow. I don't know what it is about her?" Aspanu mused.

An older carusi overheard the comment.

"Hey, donkey head, you must mean Nina. She is the best-looking girl around. She just started working here. The last girl looked like a dog. Anyway, what the hell could you do with her, you ragazzaccio, you little runt. She wants a real man like me," the older carusu announced. He flexed his muscles, making his semi-hunched back more defined. His friends laughed at his theatrical move.

"My friend does not have a donkey head, and you should watch your mouth," Carlo declared. His father had taught him never to back down from anyone. He taught him how to fight by boxing in their garden at home. Carlo had the confidence he was good with his hands, if needed.

Carlo wasn't aware fighting among carusi at the mine was strictly forbidden. The gabbelloto, Signore Modica, would beat senseless anyone who fought on mine property. That went for miners and carusi.

"Big, tough carusazzu. I'm so afraid I think I have to go take a nice shit," the older boy said. He headed for the mine, holding his ass, to visit the toilet. His friends roared with laughter.

"Carlo, are you crazy? This is our first day of work. Keep quiet and don't make trouble for us," Aspanu warned with a whisper.

"Big-shot teenager. I can take him!"

"No, you can't, and no, you won't. "

"I'm taking a quick nap," Carlo answered.

The main whistle blew, and the carusi made their way to their mine entrances. Signore Alia let out his special whistle, and Aspanu and Carlo scampered to his side.

The rest of the day was more of the same as the boys' first morning, except the smell of feces and urine was so strong, it seemed to get into the nostrils and burn the eyes.

Every time the boys came to the surface from the mine shaft, they headed with a sense of excitement to the calcaroni. Their steps were quicker in spite of the heavy weight on their shoulders. It seemed as if they were racing to get to see Nina. Neither friend wanted the other to be a step ahead, and it made the back-breaking work turn into somewhat of a game.

All day, Nina never looked up at the boys. Aspanu looked at her from the side of his head with an impish smile. Carlo took her disinterest as a challenge.

The six o'clock whistle blew when the boys were making their last trip up the mineshaft. Aspanu and Carlo nearly ran to the oven, but Nina was already gone. An old man stood in her place with the weight chart. The disappointed boys dumped their baskets and heard Alia's whistle. Their picconiere was coming out of the mine, soaked in perspiration and covered with gray dust, he was carrying his pick axe over his shoulder and the goldfinch in its cage in his other hand. The yellow bird was flitting from one side to the other side of the cage, happy to be on the surface and happy to know he would soon be among others of his species. Both boys hustled to Alia's side.

97

"A good day's work, carusi. You both did well for your first day. Tomorrow's sun rises early."

"Thank you, signore," the boys said in unison.

"Are you forgetting anything?" Alia asked.

Aspanu and Carlo looked at each other quizzically. Each boy shrugged their shoulders.

"Lanterns...you must go back down and get the lanterns," Alia ordered.

CHAPTER 21

Eleven years before Aspanu and Carlo began their daily toil through hell, John Forester Rose was kidnapped for a cash ransom by Antonino Leone.

The horrible time for the Gardner-Rose family, and the fear of losing a family member in a brutal manner did nothing to soften the owner's indiscriminate exploitation of children and miners. If the truth be told, all of the mine owners throughout Sicily became more hardened in their quest for lavish profits.

John Forester Rose was held for twenty-two days.

Hours before she was to take the ransom money to the train station in Lercara Bassa, as instructed by Antonino Leone, Elizabeth Gardner-Rose agreed to meet with Comandante Pietro Greco at Villa Lisette. Greco was concerned for the woman's safety and well-being.

Elizabeth and Greco walked around the Rose Garden, followed by two carabinieri assigned to watch over the young wife of John Forester Rose.

"Inspector, I appreciate your coming by to visit today, but I must tell you, I will not be dissuaded from taking the money to those bandits tonight. It's time this nightmare stops and my husband is returned to me."

Signora, I've known and respected your family for many years. I know that you, yourself, had to finally negotiate with Leone to save your husband, but you need to hear what you may very well be walking into," Greco stated.

"Comandante, what is on your mind?" Elizabeth asked.

"This Leone, and the men he surrounds himself with are treacherous criminals. Signore Giovanni Nicotera, our Minister of the Interior for all of Italy, has issued a shoot to kill command for these bandits. They are men with pure criminal minds. I am afraid that you are in danger if you bring the money alone. There are too many evils that lurk around these hills, and I want to see a happy ending to this story."

"You know Leone. If I go with you or any member of your department or a military escort, my husband will be killed just for spite. I cannot take that chance, Signore." Elizabeth held. She was terrified of going out at night alone, especially to the isolated train station, but she knew of no way out of the predicament which she and her husband found themselves.

"I have a suggestion, but it is strictly off the record, Signora. May I say what I need to say with your promise of secrecy?"

"Of course, Comandante. You have been very supportive of me even to the point of disagreeing with John's family on this matter. Please speak freely as time is short," Elizabeth warned.

Greco cleared his throat and spoke in a whisper. Elizabeth moved closer to the inspector to hear his words.

"I agree with you once again. When you understand the criminal mind, it is the only way to come out with your skin intact. You were bold enough to get Leone to be reasonable on his ransom demand. You understood his mentality and what he would possibly fear. Now you must use a resource of mine who will keep you out of danger, and you may never speak of this, not even to your husband. I am owed a favor from a man in this town. He is a powerful man, although in your circles, he is not important, he commands respect in Lercara Friddi and the rest of the towns around Palermo. A man of respect like him can be the intermediate between you and Leone. This man is above money, and his honor is worth more than anything to him and those in his world. Frankly, these men of honor are ashamed that this kidnapping has happened right under their noses but they don't condemn the bandits. There is a code these men of honor uphold. This man can put the word into Leone's camp that he, himself, will accompany you to the drop off. Trust me when I say this, signora, Leone, or his maniac Esposito could not hide from these men."

"And what is the cost of this protection, Comandante? My father always said to avoid these types at all cost."

"This favor that is owed me is personal. I cannot say what it was about, but suffice it to say, it will settle the score with me and this man of honor," Greco declared.

"You talk about men of honor like they truly have morals. From what I've heard, isn't this really the mafia, Comandante? I've heard this term used by my father and my in-laws from time to time. I don't think these are the kind of people with whom I should be associated."

"My dear, Signora, that word is just what it is...a word. In Sicilian, a mafiusu is a man who has boldness, swagger, confidence. A mafiusa is a beautiful woman like yourself. It's a term of endearment. I will ask you to trust me that nothing will come of this favor that is owed to me. I will talk with this man so that he may meet you. He is not much older than you, and you will immediately see he is no danger to you. This is for your protection. I give you my word."

"What is this man's name, if I may ask?" Elizabeth queried.

"His name will be given to you tonight when he arrives. And I will ask you to forget his name and not use it in the future"

"If he can help get my husband from the clutches of these brigands, I will trust your judgment, Comandante.

As darkness descended upon Villa Lisette, Elizabeth's heart began to race, her respiration quickened in anticipation.

At precisely eight-thirty, a single, two-wheeled, horse-drawn carriage with a black, folding hood appeared on the street outside Villa Lisette. Inside the chaise was a man no older than thirty years of age wearing a black, fedora hat.

As planned, Elizabeth gathered her purse and a brown, leather satchel which contained five thousand British pounds. She wore a burgundy dress that ended just above her ankles with matching shoes. Her hat was stylish but not elegant, her light blonde hair tucked neatly underneath. Elizabeth's striking features were not aided by makeup or earrings.

When she came upon the chaise, the man descended from the carriage and offered his hand.

"Good evening, Signora, I am Benedetto Di Prima. May I help you into the carriage?"

Di Prima was of medium height, strikingly handsome, with jet-black hair and large eyes to match. His smile was wide, white, and welcoming. He had a well-trimmed moustache and wore a fedora slightly cocked to the left side. The stranger wore a black, three-piece suit, a rigid, high-collar shirt with a wrap-around tie. Elizabeth felt instantly comfortable, recalling the Comandante's definition of a mafiusu. Bold, swagger, confident.

CHAPTER 22

As Domenico Alia walked to the exit of the mine property, with his pick axe over his tired shoulder, Aspanu and Carlo walked slowly to the mine entrance. They had to go down the narrow shaft and retrieve the two lanterns. The boys were totally spent from their first day as carusi.

Alia would head home to soak in a hot bath for a short reprieve from swinging the axe all day. He would eat a supper of vegetable soup and macaroni, with a piece of bread and a drizzle of olive oil, hold his son for a while, light his pipe, and prepare to retire to bed, then he would await the morning sun to start the body-punishing work all over again.

Aspanu led the way into the dark mine, feeling his way with his small, right hand scraping against the mine wall. Carlo luckily tripped over a lantern at the bottom of the first level, enabling them to see as they descended to the spot where they were working. They each grabbed a lantern by its wire handle and returned to the surface.

On the way back up, the boys saw a picconiere walking up the shaft, some sixty or seventy feet ahead of them. Carlo suddenly stopped climbing the dirt stairs, causing his friend to bump into his back.

"But Carlo, do you want to stay in this place longer? Why are we stopping?" Aspanu demanded.

"Wait...listen!" Carlo warned.

The boys could hear whimpering coming from the second level cut out.

Carlo held out a lantern and shone the light toward the large cave. There sat a carusu, his back facing the boys as he cried into his hat.

"Oh…are you okay?" Carlo said.

Aspanu raised his lantern, and the cave was fully illuminated.

The crying boy didn't turn to face the two friends. He spontaneously stopped crying.

"Mind your damned business. Get the hell away from me," the crier commanded.

Aspanu and Carlo looked at each other with dread in their eyes. Their young minds put two and two together. They knew the picconiere had done something to the crying carusu. They moved with haste up to the mine entrance and the fresh, early evening air.

Once outside, the lanterns were secured behind a large, sulfur-laced boulder, and the boys made their way from the mine to the road which led back to town.

The calcaroni kept churning and melting the day's tally, the old man who took over for Nina sat on a wooden box, plucking on a Jew's harp, emitting its monotonous pitch.

The sun had dropped in the sky, and the temperature followed. Still quite hot and humid, it was a far better feeling than the grottacalda they worked in all day.

The boys walked for a few minutes, feeling the ache in their necks from the heavy baskets they carried up the mineshaft all day. Suffering in silence, no words were spoken on their walk back home.

Suddenly, in front of the boys, appearing as if out of nowhere, four, older carusi stood blocking their path. One of them stepped in front of the others. He was the one who called Aspanu a donkey head.

Aspanu felt his empty stomach churn with the tingling he had earlier that morning. Carlo stood glaring at the leader of the pack of carusi.

"So, carusazzu, do you want to tell me to keep my mouth shut again so I can beat your ass in for you?"

Aspanu swallowed hard. Carlo responded.

"I'm not afraid of you one bit. You never should talk to my friend like that. He wasn't starting any trouble with you," Carlo blurted, showing no fear.

"We can't fight on mine property, but we can settle things here and now," the older carusu offered.

Carlo took his shoulder bag off as the older boy began getting closer.

Aspanu stood in front of his friend in defiance.

"You are not going to fight with my friend. Look, you are how old, twelve? Thirteen? How is fighting a five-year-old going to make you a man? We are all in this mine together, and even after one day, I can tell you one thing, we all have enough to worry about. Getting whipped by the gabbelloto, burned and smacked around by the picconieri, the stink. Life here is hard enough. We should never fight against each other. I'm sorry if I spoke about the girl. I meant no disrespect," Aspanu reasoned. He spoke with a maturity well beyond his years. His anxiety was not exposed.

"The kid is right, Lino, let them go," one of the four said to the leader. "They don't even have hair on their balls yet."

Lino stepped up to Aspanu. Lino was taller and thicker than Aspanu. His shoulder was hunched, revealing his veteran status as a carusu. Lino was scratching at his abdomen incessantly.

"You have balls, kid. I like you. As for your friend, try to teach him some manners. We will see each other tomorrow, and the day after, and the day after that."

"See you tomorrow. Buona notte," Aspanu offered.

The four, older carusi walked past the two younger boys. Lino rubbed Aspanu's head in a gesture of friendship.

Aspanu had saved Carlo and himself from a sure beating.

The two boys continued their long walk home to Via Cimò, albeit much slower than their pace to the mine that morning.

"You were brave, Aspanu," Carlo declared.

"I was about to shit my pants."

"I could have taken him. My father taught me 'the bigger they are the harder they fall'."

"And my father taught me to avoid fighting if possible. I used my head instead of my fists. It worked out this time."

"Somehow, between your father and my father, we will figure things out as we get older," Carlo pronounced.

The two friends walked in silence the rest of the way back to their homes.

The end of their childhood had begun.

CHAPTER 23

As the carriage pulled away slowly from Villa Lisette, Elizabeth could tell her heart was beating faster and faster, her mouth went dry, and she could feel the moisture from her hands pooling under her gloves. Di Prima, sensing her anticipation, broke the awkwardness in the carriage.

"Signora, there is nothing for you to be concerned about. I assure you that you are totally safe with me, and you will know where your husband is very soon. I can assure you he is safe," Di Prima uttered.

"Do you mean I will not see him now?" Her voice quivered from her anxiety.

"I know where he is. Within the hour he will be released in a town further north, closer to Palermo. He will be here with you by midday tomorrow.

The clicking of the horse's hooves echoed into the carriage. Di Prima kept the pace steady and as smooth as the roads would allow.

"How are you so certain, Signore Di Prima?"

"I am as sure as I am of the Sicilian blood that runs through my veins. This unfortunate business has embarrassed us as much as it has distressed you and your family. For that, I must apologize for these ruffians who have made their living without respect for genuine people such as yourself."

"I will feel better once I see my John. I can only imagine what he has been through," Elizabeth uttered. She fought back a nervous cry.

The night was very dark, as no moon or stars could be seen, due to a blanket of clouds which filled the sky. Only a lantern attached to the carriage could help guide the way on the narrow, dirt roads.

"Leone knows you are under my protection. He and his men will be like lambs."

"Forgive me, Signore Di Prima but...how do you know this? Leone, I am told, is a brutal criminal, and you seem to be a perfectly well-bred gentleman."

"Didn't you learn not to judge a book by its cover? In this country, brutality only fears brutality. What some will do for money, others find repugnant. My associates and I are true men of honor, men who are both feared and respected when we are called upon."

"Do you have a wife, Signore?"

"I do. And three small children. They are my second family, Signora."

"You were married before?"

"Never."

"I don't understand."

"Perhaps someday you will," Di Prima laughed.

The lights from the Lercara Bassa station could be seen in the distance, helping Di Prima to guide the stallion.

"Oh, my goodness. I feel a bit light-headed," Elizabeth uttered.

"Have no worry, Signora. I will talk for you. You have nothing to be concerned about. Please just breathe through your nose and stay calm. Put your trust in me."

As the carriage approached the deserted station, Di Prima pulled back gently on the reins. Elizabeth could hear her heart beating loudly in her ears. Her respiration was heavy and labored.

The carriage came to a stop in front of the station. Even the crickets were silent. Di Prima tied the horse's reins to the side of the carriage. The man of honor folded one leg over the other, he lit a cigarette and waited.

Not a minute went by when the sound of an owl hoot pierced the night. The hoot came a second time.

Di Prima returned his own whistle which sounded like a nightingale.

From behind the depot came a dark figure of a stocky man wearing a farmer's cap. The man approached the carriage with his hands open and down by his sides. Giuseppe Esposito spoke in a low and even voice. His accent was rough, his voice gravelly.

"Signore Di Prima?"

"Yes."

"Thank you for bringing the signora tonight."

"Where is your boss? I take it as an insult he sends his lieutenant," Di Prima replied. His voice was stern and cold. Elizabeth felt her heart sink and her blood go cold.

"Anto sends his respect to you. He is making sure that all things go well with Signore Rose."

"So…he hides in Sciara like a woman?"

Esposito did not respond.

Di Prima offered a cold stare to the unkempt bandit. Esposito lowered his eyes.

"At any rate, we are here to do business, as cowardly as it is."

Di Prima stepped down from the chaise. He straightened his suit, adjusted his hat, and reached into the darkened carriage for the leather satchel.

"Allura, in this bag is the agreed upon ransom of five thousand British pounds. I invite you to count it," Di Prima offered.

Esposito paused, considering the offer.

"No need, Signore Di Prima. For a man of your reputation that would be an affront," Esposito said.

"That would be true, even from a cafone like yourself. So then, I will take my piece of the bounty. I am taxing you for my involvement in this dirty affair. I am taxing you for the insult of Leone hiding like a mangy dog, and I am taxing you for your protection."

"My protection, Signore?"

"Yes. No vengeance will be taken upon you or Leone for this…this… affront. I like that word you used."

"Certainly, Signore."

"The tax equals half of the satchel. You will return with two thousand, five hundred pounds to your den. Let me say one more thing to you. If one hair is harmed on Signore Rose, there is no cave in all of Sicily in which you and Leone, and all of your men can hide."

"I understand. Mr. Rose has already been released. He was given a train ticket from Sciara to this station. If the trains are on time, he will be here by noon tomorrow.

Di Prima took his share of the ransom and left it in the bag. He placed the other half on the ground as one would drop food for a dog.

The man of honor turned and walked back to the carriage.

"Good night, Signore, and Signora," Esposito voiced awkwardly.

Di Prima turned and glared at the brigand. He climbed back up onto the carriage without a word.

Esposito scampered for the British pounds, gathering them into his shoulder bag.

Elizabeth sat speechless, her mouth agape from the proceedings. Di Prima turned the carriage to return to Lercara Friddi.

"Signora, the satchel and what is inside is yours. It is the least I can do to show our disdain for this unfortunate transaction.

"Thank you, Signore Di Prima, but what of my husband?"

"Be here at noon tomorrow. He will be on this platform. I guarantee this."

CHAPTER 24

It seemed as though the closer the two friends got to their separate homes on Via Cimò, the more they were dragging their exhausted bodies.

The early evening air on the narrow streets of Lercara Friddi blended with the aroma of simmering foods which whiffed from the windows of the apartments and houses. It was around this time of day the wooden windows, that were closed all day to keep out heat from the blaring sun, were now opened to welcome the cooler evening air. Husbands and wives chatted about their day or argued about whatever men and women bicker about. The cries of babies, the sound of pots and dishes being set around the tables added to the opera of poverty in this section of town.

This is where the workers lived. The braccianti, the laborers who used and abused their bodies in the sulfur mines and in the fields and farms, and the men who built things or tore things down.

Here lived the people who worked at the whim of the gabbelloto, or the field masters, men without feelings or compassion, for the wealthy land and mine owners. Here is where the weary workers rested while they eked out their livings, and raised their children in order to keep the cycle of rich versus poor continuing generation after generation.

Aspanu and Carlo could barely raise their arms to wave goodbye to one another as they parted to go home.

Maria Salerno was in front of her home waiting for her son, wringing her hands together. Her three other children sat on the ground, wondering why their Mama was so troubled.

Aspanu straightened his back and put a smile on his face as he approached the house. He was covered in a film of gray earth. The sweat from his brow had streaked his face from his hairline to his chin, yet he put on a face of false bravado for his mother and brothers and baby sister.

Maria, in her black, mourning dress and black, kitchen apron, brought her hands up to her quivering lips.

"Mama, good evening. I'm back from my first day of work," Aspanu announced.

"My boy has truly become the man of the family," Maria replied. "Oh, my dear God, what have I done?" She thought.

Aspanu kissed his mother. The smell of sweat and sulfur followed the fatherless family into the house. The kids scampered and waddled behind their mother and big brother to see if there would be any food this night.

"Aspanu, take off those clothes, I will wash them while you take a nice bath and then we will have some supper," Maria pronounced. No reply came from her son.

Maria turned to see Aspanu lying in a heap on the bed. His work cap still on his head, his eyes were closed. The boy was fast asleep.

Carlo opened the door to find his mother on the bed. There was no food prepared, and the other children sat quietly on the kitchen chairs, looking at nothing.

"Mama, what's wrong? Are you ill?"

Elvira didn't reply.

Carlo climbed on the bed and shook his mother.

"Mama, why are you in the bed? Shall I go for the doctor?"

Elvira, wide eyed, dressed all in black with a black turban-like kerchief tied around her head, was staring at the ceiling. A pair of black, rosary beads were intertwined tightly within her fingers.

"Mama! Mama! It's me, Carlo! Let's go! Get up, Mama!" Carlo commanded.

As if his voice woke her from a trance, Elvira's eyes focused on her son. She snapped up. She sat up quickly on the bed. She surveyed her surroundings, seeing the children sitting around the empty table.

"Holy Mother of Jesus. My dear God," Elvira shouted. She jumped from the bed, momentarily walking in circles around the room. She took pieces of wood from a pile next to the stove, shoving them into the stove to make some hot water.

"Carlo, Mama will be fine. Forgive me. I will draw the water for your bath. Give me a few minutes. Let me help you change your clothing, I will prepare something for all of us to eat, maybe some nice macaroni with peas, everything will be fine. Here, drink some lemon water, you must be thirsty from work."

Elvira was moving frantically around the room, talking but getting nothing accomplished.

Carlo walked outside to the back of the house where the family kept a vegetable garden and some chickens.

The exhausted little boy sat on a rickety, weather-beaten, wooden chair. Not long ago, his Papà would have sat on that same chair, with Carlo on his lap, singing and whistling a song or telling a story.

Carlo put his dirty hands to his face and cried like his baby brother.

CHAPTER 25

Doctor Alfonso Giordano and Monsignor Giovanni Paci were finishing their dinner. Giordano had his disappointing dinner discussion with Monsignor Paci and was attempting to make a discreet exit from the rectory.

The monsignor felt badly about rejecting Giordano's request to help improve the health and work conditions at the mines. As the monsignor had his second helping of ricotta cheese cake with several cups of mezze tazze coffee, sweetened with anisette, the doctor sipped on a glass of water with squeezed lemons. The monsignor had consumed an entire bottle of wine himself with his dinner.

 Paci tried to explain, in a convoluted way, why the sulfur mines needed to be left to the owners who had taken extraordinary risks with their investment.

"Alfonso, sulfur mines have been in the bible for thousands of years. Back then, sulfur was called brimstone, and the implications were never very good. Actually, the smell of sulfur was tied to the smell of hell. Frankly, there are some theologians who feel that death in the bowels of the earth has a divine plan. Perhaps for sins committed," Paci lectured.

"Monsignor, that is ridiculous on its face. There is no God who punishes small boys for past sins. Please tell me you do not adhere to such thinking," Giordano seethed.

"Just a theological concept, my old friend, like the concept of original sin. I did not invent these things. I simply believe."

"You know as well as I do that these gluttonous owners have turned the mines into cemeteries. These children are precious gifts who we are allowing to be suffocated daily or killed slowly by parasitic disease. For Christ's sake, these boys are not even fit for military duty when they finally turn of age. I haven't even touched upon the psychological breakdown and humiliation that befalls these children. My God, I know you for many years, Giovanni, and I know you see what I see."

Paci shook his head to get his mind clear from the alcohol he ingested.

"Your passion is admirable. Yes, I do see the problems, but I am one man rowing against the tide," Paci whispered. The monsignor didn't want to agree with the doctor and be overheard by the domestic help. In Sicily, even in the rectory, the walls had ears.

"I am warning you. Please listen to my words carefully. There is a group that is growing rapidly. They are called the Fasci Siciliani. They have been around for a few years now. They began in Catania, they spread to Messina, and as of late, they are right near us in Corleone and here in Lercara. I am treating one of their leaders of whom I will not reveal a name. This man tells me they are nearly three-hundred-thousand strong. They will not tolerate the additional taxes and higher rents that the landlords are imposing. The Fasci Siciliani wants conditions in the mines to improve. They are well aware that the health conditions are killing the men and boys who work to dig the sulfur from the earth. This group will not stop growing, and mark my words, reform is around the corner. Where will you be then monsignor?"

"My friend, and I say this with all of my deepest affection, you are a great man with a brilliant mind. My advice is for you to stick with medicine. You are treading on thin ice with this rabble Fasci Siciliani. I know from a source, which I also cannot divulge, that this group of anarchists will be short lived," Paci stated.

"God help us all, Giovanni. We find ourselves in a political snake pit that resembles Virgil and Dante in the Eighth Circle of Hell," Giordano warned.

"As the poet said of these snakes 'of weird kinds such as to remember now, still chills my blood,'" Paci quoted.

CHAPTER 26

At eleven thirty, the morning after Benedetto Di Prima accompanied Elizabeth Gardner-Rose to pay for her husband's ransom, the train station at Lercara Bassa was more crowded than normal.

There were three-people traveling to pay respects to a dead uncle in Agrigento and a newlywed couple, holding on to one another as young couples sometimes do. The lovebirds were also going to Agrigento to seek employment as teachers.

One man, dressed in a brown, three-piece suit and matching fedora, with piercing dark eyes, stood close to the tracks, smoking a short cigar.

Comandante Greco, Elizabeth Gardner-Rose, and her husband's parents, dressed formally, Mr. James Rose in a top-hat, the ladies in full, Victorian-style dresses as if they were going to a grand ball, stood on the station platform. The butler and man servant Thomas also was in attendance, as were three carabinieri in full dress uniform.

Greco surveyed the depot. His keen, law enforcement eyes slowly scanning the scene. He nodded when he saw the gentleman in the brown fedora. A smooth nod of the hat signaled the man's respect. The cigar-smoking gent was an associate of Benedetto Di Prima. He was at the station as Di Prima's eyes and ears to make certain the favor to Greco was consummated.

At twenty minutes after noon, just twenty minutes off schedule, the whistle and smoke from the steam locomotive could be seen and heard. The train was just outside of Lercara Bassa.

Elizabeth felt the butterflies in her stomach, and her heart was beating like it was the night the bounty was brought to the filthy bandit Giuseppe Esposito. This time, the anticipation was not out of fear, but excitement.

As the three-car train slowed down to pull into the station, Elizabeth stood on her toes to see into the Pullman cars, the elder Mrs. Rose clung to her husband, gently dabbing at her almost moist eyes with a lace handkerchief.

Waving from the second car, John Forester Rose looked none the worse for wear. Antonino Leone saw to it his victim was bathed, shaved, and his hair trimmed before he left for home.

John F. Rose bounded down the three steps from the train as it belched its steam ahead on the platform. He ran to his wife's arms and they embraced. Being an American, Elizabeth showed much more emotion than her husband's British parents and their man servant. Comandante Greco and his men actually showed more emotion than the stuffy Roses. Two of the policemen were actually in tears.

John gave his mother a peck on an offered cheek and shook his father's hand and off they went in a three-carriage procession to Villa Lisette. As they left the station, the fedora man acknowledged Comandante Greco with another slight tip of his hat. Di Prima and the policeman were even.

So many things occurred between the time John F. Rose was kidnapped in 1876 and Aspanu and Carlo celebrated their fourth anniversary as carusi to Domenico Alia.

A year after the ransom was paid, Antonino Leone was gunned down by the police. Some said he was set up by the men of honor, the mafia, who were gaining enormous strength in all of Sicily due to a devastating drought. If you were a farmer or landowner and you needed water for your crops, these men of honor controlled the water. Water became a commodity like any other. When there is a paucity of supply, the price only goes in one direction. Men of honor became men of lire.

Aspanu and Carlo were now nine years old and veterans of the mines. They both were suffering from symptoms of miner's anemia. The parasite caused incessant itching on their stomachs as it sucked blood from their intestines. Every Sunday afternoon, they were treated by Doctor Giordano at no charge. The parasite would return shortly after the doctor got it under control. The mine owners did nothing to improve the sanitary conditions in the mines. Both Aspanu and Carlo were already showing signs of skeletal deformity, the half-hump back.

Piccionere Alia had two more children. Both boys, who made him having to work even harder for his family. As he picked away at the mine walls, the number of baskets the boys had to carry increased year after year. Aspanu and Carlo would have to work at least until they were fourteen to pay back the soccorso di morti, owed to Alia.

Carlo's Mama, still suffering from depression, nearly lost her children to the foundling home. Maria Salerno helped her to keep her family intact. It was clear Elvira's next son in line would be working as a carusu in the sulfur mine.

Maria was no longer wearing her black dress. She was seeing a married man from a town a few miles away from Lercara Friddi.

Monsignor Paci stayed the course of his Archbishop. There was no interference with commerce in Lercara Friddi from the rectory at Santa Maria Della Neve.

The Gardner-Rose family sold their business. The mines were now owned by a variety of owners: Romano, Gonzales, Sartorio, Sociale, Giordano, and others.

The Fasci Siciliani were making their move to have major demonstrations in several mining towns throughout Sicily. Giovanni Giolitti left in disgrace because of a banking scandal. Francesco Crispi, the Sicilian, was again Prime Minister of Italy in mid-December of 1893. Crispi turned out to be different than the sulfur mine workers and farmers had hoped.

Nina was now nearly thirteen.

Pippo Furnari speaking to a class of
children regarding the history of Sicily

Classroom of Children

Meeting the mayor of Lercara Friddi

Brainstorming with historian in
Lercara Friddi City Hall

Carusi I interviewed who spent
35 years below ground

Exterior Sulfur Mine Entrance

Authentic Basket Used to
Carry Ore by Carusi

Stairs Leading Down Into Sulfur Mine

Sulfur Ore

CHAPTER 27

As Aspanu and Carlo passed their fourth-year anniversary as carusi, the one and only positive thing they achieved at the sulfur mine was getting Nina Miceli to acknowledge them at the calcaroni.

A smile, sometimes a wave, from Nina gave the two infatuated carusi a bit of a respite after each load of earth was dumped for processing.

As repulsive as the stench of human waste and perspiration was, as horrible as the heat, as it neared one hundred and twenty degrees, as dreadful as the lack of fresh air was, as atrocious as what these two little boys witnessed how some of the picconieri abused the carusi, Nina gave them the one thing they needed more than anything. Nina gave Aspanu and Carlo hope.

Some of the older carusi would say appalling things about the young girl with the big eyes and new, bouncy tits. Some of the carusi would whistle as they approached the calcaroni to get Nina's attention, but she always kept her eyes on the scales and her papers. Quite often, Carlo was ready to drop his basket of sulfur-laden rocks and fight for Nina's honor, but Aspanu would somehow defuse the situation.

Both Aspanu and Carlo had fallen in love with Nina. She was more than just a fantasy. Nina had become someone the boys adored, albeit for a minute or two, fifteen or twenty times a day. Each load of sulfur gave them a glimpse of her beauty. If Nina happened to glance in the direction of Aspanu and Carlo that was enough to keep them climbing up the mine shafts in the hope she would grin at them.

On the rare occasion Nina would smile, showing her beautiful white teeth against her dark skin, the two pals would get a fluttering feeling in their stomachs and loins which was as close to bliss as they could imagine.

For four years, Nina was the only thing in Aspanu and Carlo's world that was truly beautiful.

Aspanu was the first to vocalize his feelings. It was a day the rain was coming down so hard the weight of the basket seemed to double. On the way up from the mine shaft on their third load is when the two boys' first real argument took place.

"One day I will marry her," Aspanu blurted.

"Marry who?" Carlo queried.

"Nina! I will marry her one day."

"Are you crazy?   Marry Nina? What would she want with a carusu like you?

"I can see it in her eyes. She likes me," Aspanu boasted.

"She doesn't know if you're alive or dead. Dozens of boys pass her way many times a day. And you think she likes you? What makes you so special?" Carlo demanded.

"You are jealous because she smiled at me."

"She smiled at you? It was me she was smiling at, you idiot."

"Trust me when I tell you she likes me better than you, and when I get old enough to marry her, I will."

"You are the dumbest carusu in all of Sicily. Marry Nina? First of all, you are too poor for her, and she will want a man who can provide for her."

"Soon I will be out of this stupid mine and do something that will make a lot of money," Aspanu bragged.

"Soon, my ass. Signore Alia owns you. And he will continue to own you for a long time. But, I will be out of here and make a name for myself. By the time you get out of here, I will already be married to Nina," Carlo replied.

"You? That makes me laugh. How do you intend to do that? Take Signore Modica's job? You are being ridiculous, Carlo. And how will you get to marry her first, Carlo? You are becoming a twisted mess," Aspanu seethed.

"And you are a short, stupid-looking…"

"Just answer my question. How will you get to marry her before me?"

"That's my business. But it won't be by carrying a basket of dirt all day," Carlo declared.

"Nonsense. You sound very stupid. Maybe you will become the Mayor of Lercara Friddi and take Sartorio's job from him?" Aspanu laughed.

"I am going to work at the union," Carlo bragged.

"The union? What union, you fool?"

"Fasci Siciliani. They will make big changes for all the workers. Here in this hell and in the fields, so the farmers can eat, too," Carlo preached.

"And how do you know all this?"

"I've gone to a few of their secret meetings. I didn't tell you because you would have made fun of me. Your ideas about things are different than mine."

"How am I different?" Aspanu asked.

"I'm a fighter. I stand up for myself. You are afraid. All you like to do is talk."

"No, it's not that I'm afraid. I just can't see the sense in fighting all the time. If this union of yours wants to fight, then you will lose. I'm smart enough to know that the owners of the land and the sulfur mines are very strong. And the government is even stronger."

"The Fasci tried talking first. Nobody listened. Aspanu, how many carusi have we seen carried out of the mine? How many boys do we know who just never came back to work because later we heard that they were dead? You've seen with your own eyes picconieri beating their carusi. Sometimes very badly. And you've seen boys being raped by their bosses. We are still boys, but I feel like an old man," Carlo lectured.

"My dream will come true. I will get out of here one day soon, get a good job, ask to be married to Nina. Wait until I am old enough and get married to her. I don't care about your stupid union and trying to save the world. Will the union help put bread on my table? Will they help with my sicknesses? My baby brother will soon be a carusu, like yours will. And if they are unlucky and don't find a good man like Signore Alia, it will be their cries that we hear as some miner is fucking them in their ass," Aspanu lamented.

"I would stick a pick deep in his skull if he hurt my baby brother."

"I thought you would go to your Fasci Siciliani for help. They don't care either. I heard some of the picconiere talking. They said the Fasci are communists, or anarchists. I don't know what that is but it sounded bad."

"First, we are arguing over Nina, now the Fasci, but you will see, I will have my union and my Nina... in time."

"Only if I am dead and buried, Carlo. Dead and buried, my friend."

CHAPTER 28

It was December 15th, 1893. There was turmoil throughout all of Sicily. Demonstrations for lower taxes. Better pay and better working conditions turned the Fasci Siciliani dei lavoratori, the Sicilian Workers League, into a movement with an incredible following and momentum. Riots had broken out across the entire island.

An emergency meeting was held in Palermo at the headquarters of General Roberto Morra di Laviano, the aristocrat commandante of the XII Corpo D'Armata.

At the meeting were the mayors of several towns in the province, including Giuliano Sartorio, the mayor of Lercara Friddi, Vincenzo Colmayer, the Prefect of Palermo, and his Vice Prefect, Giuseppe Sorce Nola, and Comandante Greco.

The specially invited guests of the meeting met in an anteroom just outside of General Morra's office. The guests mostly knew each other from various political events that took place in the past, but few were very familiar with Morra as a person. He was, however, known by his no-nonsense reputation. Everyone shook hands and exchanged mundane pleasantries before an aide to the general opened his office door.

The general's office was stark, with plain, brown walls like a military barracks. A large, pine table with simple, brown, wooden chairs were placed around the table. Detailed maps of Sicily and the Province of Palermo were on the wall next to the general's plain desk, which resembled a common teacher's school desk. Morra himself was in a full, blue and tan military uniform, with medals running down his ample chest. His cap had a fine, black, leather bill with a single, blue star affixed to the front. Shiny black boots ran up just under his knees. The general was tall, over six feet, with blue eyes and close, cropped, light blond and gray hair. He had the fair looks of a northerner.

A worker had just replaced an oil painting of outgoing Prime Minister Giovanni Giolitti, who just resigned after a scandal, with a large photograph of Francesco Crispi, the new and former Prime Minister.

Morra started the meeting in the smoke-filled room.

"Gentleman, I was in Rome last night and met with the new Prime Minister. I have been appointed as Special Commissioner with full military and civil powers over all of Sicily. Signore Crispi has given me firm and specific orders. We are to arrest any and all of the insurrectionists who have created the unrest of recent months. The towns of Corleone and Lercara Friddi are clearly the towns that have been identified as the next major targets of the Fasci Siciliani. Corleone for the farmland and Lercara for the sulfur mines. Any sympathizers or members of this gang are to be arrested and brought to a summary trial. Any worker's associations are to be immediately dissolved and disbanded. As you all know, we have been plagued by numerous demonstrations throughout Sicily. The government has been petitioned by the largest landowners and mine owners in Sicily to help quell the unrest. Just a few days ago, government buildings, a flour mill, and a major bakery were burned to the ground because they refused to lower prices. Five days ago, eleven peasants were killed in a demonstration in Giardinello because of the socialist-inspired protests. We can go on and on about these Fasci Siciliani disrupting our government and the economy. So far, hundreds of demonstrators have been killed for their unfortunate and, as of now, illegal cause. They have even turned the peasants away from the church, blaming the priests for siding with the landlords and mine owners. This must be stopped, and it must be stopped now. Are there any questions so far?"

"Yes, General, I have a few questions. You say an arrest and a summary trial. Under what conditions can a person be detained and given the summary trial?" Mayor Sartorio asked. Sartorio was known to be an avid protector of the land barons and mine owners. There were rumors his arc-rival, Signore Nicolosi, tolerated the Fasci Siciliani. He had plenty of reasons to ask this question. Family members of Sartorio, and perhaps the mayor himself owned a large mine in Lercara Friddi.

"I will ask Prefect Colmayer to address this question, as this is under his authority," Morra answered.

"Gentlemen, any person who is suspected of participating or sympathizing with the Fasci and their demonstrations will be subject to arrest and immediate trial," Colmayer replied.

"And what proof is required, sir?" Sartorio queried.

"Excellent question, Signore Mayor. The accused may be charged based on simple statements without evidence. All union leaders, workers, and any who have been in the demonstrations are subject to arrest. Statements from mayors, carabinieri, anyone in authority, can bring these charges to the prefect's office," Colmayer explained.

Comandante Greco raised his hand as was recognized by Colmayer.

"May I ask where these protesters will be kept? I must inform you that in Lercara, we do not have adequate jails for this kind or roundup," Greco announced.

General Morra cleared his throat to focus the meeting back to him.

"You will commandeer any government building and school to jail these anarchists and their followers. After trial, they will be taken to Palermo and kept there in the Carcere Della Ucciardone penitentiary.

The insurrectionists will be held in Palermo or sent to one of our island prisons. Look gentlemen, I have been advised that there are nearly two hundred Fasci have been established on this island. This organization is less than three years old and has grown like a plague over Sicily. The days of allowing this nonsense to spread under Giolitti are over. Prime Minister Crispi will squash this rebellion, and by this time next year, the Fasci Siciliani will be a mere memory."

"And how many men do you have to accomplish this extraordinary task, General?" Greco asked.

"Forty thousand at the moment. More if need be, Comandante. I called up these reservists to shut down these so-called workers' unions as quickly as possible. Under my authority, summary executions will be used when we deem it necessary. We will not go easy on the leaders of the Fasci. I will be passing around the names of these wanted men.

"Signore Colmayer, as Prefect, may I ask what the sentences will be?" Sartorio asked. His mind was racing as he considered who of his political rivals would be charged.

"A minimum of five years at hard labor. Other sentences will be commensurate with their involvement in the Fasci. Those terms will be up to twenty years or so," Colmayer responded quickly.

"And what of women demonstrators? I hear that women in some towns are a force to be reckoned with," Greco asked.

"They will be treated the same as men. Summary trial as well as execution if need be. The people will know we are serious when women are jailed or shot," Colmayer blurted.

The General spoke again. "And those who wear the uniform or red rosettes of the Fasci will be treated especially harsh by my officers."

"We all know who the troublemakers are in Lercara. I will have those names on your desk in the morning, prefect," Sartorio promised.

"Mayor, the Vice-Prefect, Signore Sorce will be taking up residence in Lercara. He has my full support and will speak with me via telegram on a daily basis. The general assures me that his word will be met quickly with the militia," Colmayer pronounced.

"Trust me, gentleman. My officers have been given the authority to shoot into the crowds if necessary. Our soldiers are well trained to follow their orders," Morra declared.

CHAPTER 29

Aspanu and Carlo, friends literally since their cribs, walked to the sulfur mine for another lengthy and horrible day. It was still dark at nearly six o'clock in the morning. Their physical and emotional stress of being carusi, sold into slavery by their mothers to a piccionere, had taken its toll after four, long years of hard labor.

There was no happiness in these boys. They walked with their gaze to the dusty earth, never smiling, always with their stare fixed and without spirit behind their eyes. The carusi spent most of their time below ground, not unlike moles who dug deep into the ground for grubs and other lowly insects.

Of late, Aspanu and Carlo didn't speak much to each other as they walked from and to Via Cimò. Their mutual affection toward the beautiful Nina had put them at odds as competitors with each other.

"My Mama said that there is trouble ahead with the Fasci. Everyone in town is talking about it. Anyone involved with the union will be thrown in jail or shot like they were at other mines," Aspanu declared.

"And why are you telling me this?" Carlo asked. His voice expressed a mind your own business tone.

"Just be careful, Carlo. You could get into bad trouble or maybe even hurt."

"How can it be worse than the life we are living?" Carlo asked.

"Prison is living?"

"Slavery is living?" Carlo responded.

"My Mama said..." Aspanu started but was interrupted by his friend.

"And I heard my Mama talking to another woman who said your Mama has a boyfriend, so shut up," Carlo blurted

Aspanu felt a surge of anger run up into his chest.

"Never! You are saying this to get to me. You know I like Nina, and you are being evil."

"Nina will be with me. I am going to be somebody important with the Fasci someday. You will see! Signore Verra shook my hand and told me to keep the fight going and not to be afraid," Carlo declared.

"You'd better not let Signore Modica hear you talk like this. He will split your head like a melon. He said the Fasci will be all arrested and sent to prison, and if anyone..."

"Up your ass with that monster, Modica. He will be the first to go, I promise you that," Carlo shouted.

"Quiet, Carlo. I don't want to be part of this. Somebody will hear you and think I'm also a Fasci."

Domenico Alia was walking slowly toward the entrance of the mine. He looked tired, and his head was lowered. The boys quickened their pace to catch up with him.

"Buongiorno, signore," Aspanu said.

Alia turned his head slowly and mumbled something.

"Are you ill, signore?" Aspanu asked.

"My children have the influenza. I was awake all night with my wife trying to comfort them. The little one has a fever and it looks grave according to Doctor Giordano. The child is very weak," Alia replied.

"Shouldn't you be home with them?" Carlo queried.

"Home? I can't afford to be sick and to stay home. And mark my words, if you two don't pick up the pace today and make your mark by mid-afternoon, I swear I will put my bare foot in both of your asses."

Carlo glanced at Aspanu and frowned. Alia had never hit them or beat them or ever talked that harshly to them before this moment.

"We will work as hard as ever, signore," Aspanu exclaimed.

"Good! Perhaps I can leave a bit early if you do. Now let's get to work," Alia mumbled.

Down into the mine the trio went, the boys carrying their lanterns, Alia carried his axe and the bird cage. They were way down into the mine, in the sixth level, after the years of sweat and toil. The level they were working on was over five hundred feet below ground. Even this early in the morning, the heat was already oppressive, and breathing was more difficult than ever.

As they passed the third level, the picconiere Vincenzo Dolce had his usual lurid comments toward Alia and his two boys.

"Ohhh, Domenico! I lost one of my carusi yesterday. The hookworm seems to have gotten through his guts. I have only two as you do and I need a third to have some fun with. How about we make a deal? A trade maybe? Or some cash?" Dolce asked.

"I would rather slit my own throat. You will never take one of my carusi. Besides, I made a deal with their mothers that they would work together always, and I am a man of my word," Alia replied. He shuffled Aspanu and Carlo in front of him.

"I hear your kids are sick. Maybe you will change your mind if you need money to bury them," Dolce said.

Alia ignored the insult and moved down the shaft toward his level.

When they reached the sixth level, Alia placed his axe against his thigh, spit into his hands, raised his tool high over his head, and crashed it into the wall in anger. Aspanu and Carlo waited for the stones to fall and gather them into their baskets.

Alia began to sing the song he sang hundreds of times before. It was the miner's refrain, Vitti 'Na Crozza:

I saw a skull
I saw a skull on a stone block
And with this skull I started talking.
He replied with a great sorrow:
I died without a single toll of bell.

All my years passed very soon,
They passed and went away, I don't know where;
Now that I've reached the age of eighty,
I call the skull and nobody responds.

What will I do of my life, now?
I'm not able to work anymore.
This life is all made of pain
And in this way, I can't live anymore.

Prepare with flowers my bed
Since I've reached the end of my life.
Time has come for my rest,
I leave this nice world and leave everything.

Aspanu and Carlo knew the words by heart but never sang them. Alia sang in a somber and quivering voice. Dolce's words had affected him, almost to tears.

Suddenly, there was a blood-curdling scream that came from above them in the shaft. Alia dropped his pick axe and bolted up the narrow shaft, hitting his shoulder against a wall. Aspanu and Carlo were on his heels, choking on the dust the piccionere left in his wake.

Other picconieri had also started running toward the higher level.

Alia reached a crowd of picconieri and carusi who stood around the slumped body of Vincenzo Dolce. He was sitting naked against the mine wall.

Dolce was dead. His eyes were open and back into his head. His mouth was open, blood pouring out onto his gray, dust-covered chest.

A small hand pick was buried into the back of Dolce's skull.

CHAPTER 30

With Vitti 'Na Crozza still ringing in their ears, Aspanu and Carlo stood with the rest of the carusi and picconieri looking at the dead body of Signore Dolce.

One of the other picconieri sent his carusu to summon the gabbelloto, Signore Modica. Soon, there would be a real monster on the scene.

Aspanu and Carlo had never seen a dead body like Dolce. They had seen miners and carusi collapse and be taken from the mines only to discover later they had died. Never a murdered body. The boys were fascinated with death, as it was a real possibility every day of their lives. Cave ins, explosions, fires and disease were always a possibility. Fortunately, their bird Beppe was still chirping and jumping from one side of the cage to the other, so no one had died from sulfur gas. The boys stood fixated on the scene. Dolce's blood had stopped oozing from his mouth and nose. One of the picconieri pointed out Dolce's penis was erect. A comment was made about his manhood, but no one laughed. Someone said lust for the angels. No one laughed.

Cowering in the corner of the cave was a carusu who stood staring at his victim. The boys knew him as Turo. He was quite older, perhaps sixteen or seventeen, but it was hard to tell his true age. Turo was twisted like an Easter biscotti. His left shoulder was six inches down from his right shoulder, a hump back practically hiding his thick neck. Turo had suffered from a bad case of rickets, a result of poor nutrition, so his legs were bowed, making him much shorter than most of the other carusi. The teen's legs were badly marked from the result of being whipped by Dolce's belt and burned by the miner's lamp.

Domenico Alia approached the quivering carusu. Alia knelt next to the short boy. He could see the blood that had splattered on Turo's arms and chest.

"Son, what is your name? Do you know your name?" Alia queried.

"Yes, I am Arturo Giovanni Bucaro," Turo answered.

"Why did you kill your piccionere?"

"He deserved worse. I should now go and kill his entire family," Turo mumbled. His gaze never left his victim.

"Please, Arturo. Was he beating you badly?" Alia asked.

"He beat me almost every day of my life. After awhile, the stick and the belt didn't even hurt. He burned me with the lamp if he felt like laughing. My cousin is dying from the hookworm, and he still beat him. He raped him and me at his whim. I can hardly move my bowels anymore. I wish I could have burned him inch by inch or ripped his skin from his body," Turo said. His monotone, matter-of-fact cadence made Alia's skin crawl.

Suddenly, Signore Modica was standing in front of the gathered crowd of boys and men who were watching the melodramatic scene.

"Holy Mother of baby Jesus! Who killed this man?" Modica bellowed.

Domenico Alia stood aside from Turo, exposing the answer to the squat, seething gabbelloto. Turo paid no mind to the feared mine boss, still staring wide-eyed at his handiwork.

Modica took the wide, three-foot long, leather barber's belt he hung from his waist belt. The gabbelloto wore a belt and suspenders which exenterated his barrel chest and ample belly.

"You son of a whore!" Modica hollered. His voice boomed off the mine walls, sending a shiver down everyone's spine.

The enraged gabbelloto approached Turo and raised the belt over his shoulder to strike the cowering teen.

Alia, taller, leaner, and stronger than Modica grabbed the barber belt in mid-air before the mine boss could whip Turo.

"What are you doing, you piece of shit? This boy needs to be beaten to within an inch of his life before I drag him out of here to the carabinieri. Get out of my way you dog!" Modica screamed.

"Leave him alone. He did what he had to do. He took his vengeance," Alia hissed.

"Vengeance, you say? I don't give two fucks about this dead piece of shit. If he wanted to kill him, he should have done it somewhere else. God, damn it, he has shut down my job. I can't have this," Modica blurted. He sounded like a madman, his eyes were twice their normal, beady size with rage.

"If you call the carabinieri, the mine will be shut the entire day, and none of us will make a wage," one of the picconieri offered.

"So what am I supposed to do, you stupid morons?"

"Nothing!" Alia blurted. You do nothing. You go back to your other work. Only this mine knows of this. We leave this piece of garbage here for the rest of the day. At the end of the day we make it as if a wall came down on him," Alia suggested.

"Either way, his family can't get him buried from the church, and who cares anyway?" another miner said.

"We are all sworn to silence. No one will know better," Alia offered.

"And what about this piece of shit carusu that killed him?" Modica asked.

"Now he and the other boy are free from the soccorso di morti. They can go away from this place and start another life," Alia answered.

"So what stops any carusi from killing their bosses to stop working? That is insane!" Modica yelled.

"This is our lot in life. Everyone knows this is our destiny. When was the last time this happened? Never! Dolce deserved what he got. Now we make it look like an accident," Alia replied.

Signore Modica, the brutal gabbelloto, all at once realized the reasoning of Alia was a good solution for all involved.

"Agreed then. Now everyone...get back to work. I will not tolerate one basket less than yesterday. I don't care if you all have to work sixteen hours today. Make sure not one gram less than yesterday. Understood?" Modica bellowed.

The men and boys nodded in agreement.

"And you...Alia...I leave this is your hands. Drag this piece of shit up after the last whistle. Then I'll report the accident. And then come to my office when this is all over with," the gabbelloto commanded.

"Yes, signore. Have no further concern," Alia replied.

Modica turned on his heels and began climbing up the mine shaft.

One of the miners threw a stained, sulfur-smelling piece of tattered burlap over Dolce's head and torso.

Alia approached the still, now almost catatonic, Turo.

"Allura, Arturo. Work with me for the rest of the day. You and your sidekick can leave the mine with the rest of the crowd, and no one will be the wiser. Then make your way into the hills for a while. Maybe find some work in another town. Send word to me where you are, and I will send for you when the time is right. Maybe you will not even want to return here. Say nothing about this to anyone, ever. Understood?" Alia pronounced.

Turo looked up at Alia. He understood everything.

The murdering carusu's eyes welled with tears, his lips quivering from emotion.

"Sa, benedica," Turo managed to whimper.

"God bless you, too, Arturo," Alia replied.

The custodian of the only elementary school in Lercara Friddi, Pietro Lentini, had lost a father and an older brother in the mines when he was a boy. He had never forgotten the wails of his grandmother, mother, aunts and sister the day his father and forty-six other men and carusi perished. Some of the dead, one being his father, were dragged from the mine. They all died soon after. No funeral was allowed by the church because of the violent death they suffered.

He and Francesco Piazza were classmates until Lentini had to leave school in the fifth grade when he lost his father. Luckily for Lentini, he did not have to work as a carusu in the sulfur mines. Instead, Lentini worked for an uncle, his father's brother, who used the young boy to help in his small construction business. Lentini and Piazza remained close friends, even though Piazza went on to high school and then to the University of Palermo to study political science. Piazza always felt badly for the underdog, and Lentini was no exception. Pietro didn't pity his friend Lentini as he knew he himself would have also had to quit school to work and help the family, if anything would have happened to his father, who was also a sulfur miner.

Piazza had taken to the works of Karl Marx, Friedrich Engels, Paul Lafargue, and other champions of socialism. Piazza became a closet atheist, to appease his parents, rather than embarrass them. Pietro had no idea of his friend's politics and religious views until they both became men and had families. Piazza had great respect for his childhood buddy and made sure he never looked down upon Pietro's lack of education and sophistication.

When the now Fasci Siciliani leader, Francesco Piazza, met with Lentini in a quiet tavern one morning and began talking about the Fasci cause to demand better working conditions, lower taxes, and higher wages in the sulfur mines and farms, Lentini committed to his old friend to take his revenge upon the elite land and sulfur mine owners.

Several meetings were held surreptitiously in the basement of the school, where only a group of about twenty Fasci members were invited.

Six days before Christmas in 1893, Piazza asked Lentini to allow a meeting at the school for the Lercara Fascio.

"Pietro, tomorrow evening we need to have an emergency meeting at the school. Can you arrange for it?" Piazza implored.

"Anything for you and the cause, Francesco. Of course. May I ask what the emergency is all about?" Lentini asked.

"The Fascio wants to put together a large demonstration of workers. We want to plan the event tomorrow night. Bernardino Verro, the leader from Corleone, has agreed to join us and review our demands," Piazza advised.

"He may be the most important Fasci leader in all of Palermo province. I heard him speak at a meeting in Corleone not long ago. I didn't understand everything he was saying, but he was very passionate and impressive," Lentini stated.

"He is indeed, but I must tell you, he and I do not always see eye-to-eye on some things. This meeting can turn into a battle of sorts. It usually ends with us agreeing to disagree. If the truth be told, and I would say this to only you my dear friend, Verro was part of the Fratuzzi, the Little Brothers Mafiosi in Corleone. He was with them until only two or three months ago, for his own protection. Now, he says they are his arch enemies. Verro changes sides like you change your shirt, Pietro."

"I understand, Francesco. I will make the side door of the school open for seven in the evening. Is that suitable?" Lentini asked.

"Perfect. I will advise the others. Thank you for your loyalty to the cause. Things are quite dangerous for us now. The Vice Prefect has taken an apartment in town. He is watching us, and we are watching him. It's a cat and mouse game. We are the mice."

Just before seven the night of December 19th, when Vice Prefect Giuseppe Sorce was taking a bath in his apartment and preparing for dinner later that evening, the Fascio members began filing into the school, one at a time. The members were covered by darkness, all taking roundabout walks to assure they weren't followed. One slip-up and they would all be arrested, or worse.

By seven, all of the members of the Fascio were present and accounted for, including Piazza and Lentini. The members spoke in low tones, using a few candles to illuminate the basement room of the school. No smoking was allowed so as not to leave the stench of cigars and cigarettes smoke in the building.

At seven fifteen, Bernardino Verro came in through the door with two of his loyal associates from the Fascio in nearby Corleone. They had come to Lercara Friddi by donkey.

Verro, a tall, distinguished-looking man, dressed formally in a suit and tie, removed his hat and waded into the Fascio members of Lercara Friddi. Verro recalled them all by name, shook each of their hands with both of his, along with a warm embrace.

The room was stark, student desks were piled on one wall, brooms and mops on the other. The men all stood, as there were no adult chairs available. A winter chill filled the room, no wood would be burned for warmth so as not to attract attention at that time in the evening. Everyone wore a coat and hat, some of the members wore gloves. The meeting would not take very long, as creature comforts were nil.

"Thank you all for coming. I will dispense with the salute to the King to get the meeting moving quickly. I want to thank Signore Verro and his seconds for being gracious enough to join our meeting, as his opinion in valued here," Piazza began.

"I am appreciative of the invitation and hope that we can help in any way possible," Verro replied.

"Most in this room want to have an immediate demonstration which will shut down the mines for the day. The farm workers will put down their plows and not place any seeds for the day. It is time that we have our demands heard by this new Crispi government and show everyone in high office we mean business. The Sartorio and Nicolosi factions must be banned from running this town once and for all. Both of these families have no regard for the working-class people and are only in power to control the economy and line their own pockets. They must be removed immediately," Piazza declared.

Verro raised his arm to speak.

"Gentlemen, if you don't mind an opposing opinion. We are in a very difficult position for a demonstration at this moment in time. Prime Minister Crispi, although he comes from our island, has made it very clear that any demonstrations will be met with by force. Our intelligence committee has informed us of a large militia, under the leadership of General Morra, that will repel any and all rallies with the strongest of replies. We do not attack tax tollhouses in Corleone. Never! Our Fascio thinks it is counter-productive and frankly, too dangerous. The military has been ordered to shoot to kill, to shoot into the crowds of workers to end any march against the establishment. I strongly advise to postpone any protest for the time being."

"They wouldn't dare fire into the crowd of workers so close to Christmas. I would argue that a demonstration is both necessary and timely. Our people are starving, and many will not make it through another winter. The recent taxation has proven the government's lack of compassion and understanding of the plight of all workers," Piazza countered.

"General Morra has been ordered to quell the Fasci. He is a man who follows orders to the letter. His men are trained militia who believe that what we are proposing will destroy the economy in Sicily and the mainland. I implore you to retreat to fight for another day. As I see it, the Fasci Siciliani will be defeated and disbanded after the New Year if we are not prudent," Verro pleaded.

The argument went on for over an hour. The room began to get colder as the evening progressed.

Piazza and the men in his Fascio seemed to lean toward postponement of the demonstration. Verro and his associates, thinking they had won the argument, bid their farewells and returned to Corleone.

A bitter disagreement among the Lercara Friddi Fascio members ensued after Verro departed. Piazza won in the end.

A mass demonstration was planned for December 25th, Christmas day, in the town square under the shadow of the church of Santa Maria Della Neve.

CHAPTER 31

Nina Miceli had become a young woman. It had been four years since her Papà was killed along with Aspanu and Carlo's fathers in the Gardner-Rose mine collapse.

It took awhile for the trauma of Signore Miceli's death to subside enough for Nina to be able to even speak a word. The ordeal of her father's sudden death still affected the now thirteen-year old girl.

When she neared her monthly menstruation, Nina's temperament teetered between crying and rage. She would often think of her Papà and inexplicably burst into tears. Her anger was usually taken out on her mother and younger sister, especially when she saw some girls her age going to school. Nina had loved going to school, but left in the third grade to work at the Gardner-Rose mine.

"This is your monthly curse, cara Nina. Some of us call it a curse, others may call it their monthly friend. You must think of it as your friend for the rest of your life, and it may go easier on you," the widow Signora Miceli would always say to her budding daughter.

Nina worked at the calcaroni, logging in the endless trail of the carusi who dumped their baskets of sulfur-laced stones into the designated bins. She worked from dawn to dusk for pennies a day to help her mother put food on the table for her fatherless family.

As her breasts began to develop, the carusi would stare as they passed by her station. Some of the older boys would whistle her way or say things that truly frightened her.

"Look boys, Nina has a big pimple on her cheek. That means only one thing," an older carusi once said, mortifying Nina, driving the tears from her eyes.

Nina kept her shoulders rounded all day in order to hide her budding breasts. She wanted them, and herself for that matter, to be invisible to the world. All Nina knew from her mother always telling her, boys and men, "only want one thing." Nina had no real idea about what the "thing" actually was.

The new teenage girl had no real idea about how pregnancy worked but was frightened by it nonetheless. Her Mama didn't explain things to her, except to show Nina how to use the clean, white clothes inside her underpants.

Nina now understand what the carusi meant when they said she had the rag on, which would make her olive skin blush and her tears roll down her pretty cheeks.

Aspanu and Carlo both had always thought Nina was ignoring their glances and smiles, but Nina did indeed notice them. She actually looked forward to seeing them, through the quick, almost imperceivable glances she took at the two carusi friends. Nina thought they were both simpatici, cute, little boys who seemed different than most of the other, more forward carusi. They seemed somehow gentler and better behaved than the other mine boys.

For their part, Nina was a fantasy. Not in a sexual way, since the two friends only knew their penis' were for peeing at their age. Nina was a fantasy to both of them because she was pretty and quiet and would one day become their wife, a person to cook and clean and take care of the garden and babies. They knew nothing about making a baby, except from what they heard from the lurid remarks the older boys would make.

Carlo would always be the one of the two friends who was bold enough to say "buongiorno" or "buon pomeriggio" or "buona sera" or comment on the weather to get Nina's attention. Carlo's quick comments were largely ignored, save for a grin or an occasional smile. Her occasional quiet reactions would provide incentive for the boys to bring their heavy loads to the calcaroni. After four years, they still had an extra bit of speed in their walk, holding their shoulders upright when they approached the oven. In her own way, Nina was a breath of fresh air, interrupting their hellish existence. She could never know the importance of what her presence meant to Carlo and Aspanu.

Of late, Signora Miceli warned her daughter often, never to speak or even listen to anyone who would talk to her about the Fasci Siciliani.

"They will steal your soul. You will lose your job. You will be thrown in prison and raped by the militia if you are accused of being around the Fasci. Then they will come for your sister and me," Nina's Mama preached.

The word rape was frightful even though Nina didn't truly understand it. All she could imagine was something being forced into her vagina or culo. That idea sent endless shivers of fear up Nina's spine.

On the day piccionere Dolce was killed, Nina knew something had happened within the mine. Dolce's bin remained empty while Domenico Alia's bin was being filled by two of Dolce's carusi along with Aspanu and Carlo.

Nina could tell by the looks on the carusi faces something was not quite right. They were much more somber than ever before.

Signore Modica was spending more of his time around that particular mine, slapping his thick barber's belt hard onto the side of his leg as he shouted out orders for the carusi to move faster and hustle back down into the mine.

"Porca miseria, you will taste the belt on your backs if I see you lagging," Modica would bellow.

Curiosity got the better of Nina. She decided to find out what was happening in that mine.

Uncharacteristically, Nina waited for Aspanu and Carlo as they approached the calcaroni. Nina put her two fingers and thumb together mouthing words to the two friends. "Chi successi?" But what goes? to the two friends. She shrugged her shoulders in the sign of a question.

Aspanu looked at Carlo was who was usually the one who would always speak up. Carlo lowered his eyes to the ground in mute silence.

"Nothing, just very hot down there today," Aspanu finally replied. He too lowered his gaze to the ground. Nina knew something was amiss.

There was communication between Aspanu, Carlo, and Nina. The ice was broken.

CHAPTER 32

Maria, her husband dead for years, was very lonely. She met a cousin of Benedetto Di Prima, one Salvatore Todaro, at Doctor Giordano's office one day when she brought her youngest son to be treated for an infected foot. Todaro was visiting Giordano to bring medicine to his pregnant wife.

Todaro was known to every mafia family in the entire region as a man of respect and a man who was vicious and deadly when he needed to be.

Todaro was smitten by Maria. He would see Maria again as she walked to the market or ran other errands. Todaro made idle talk at first, then he became outright flirtatious. It wasn't long before Todaro rented an apartment from an old widow, who was sworn to secrecy, for his assignations with Maria.

Maria would ask her mother or aunt to watch her children as she had chores to do. Both women knew what Maria was doing but not with whom. No words were ever said, and no questions were ever asked.

During one of their weekly rendezvous, Maria and Tò, as he was called, shared some pillow talk.

"Tò, I am so happy I met you, so please, take no offense at what I am about to say to you," Maria whispered.

"There is nothing you can say to me that would be offensive, my love," Todò said. He kissed her head which was nestled into his chest.

"I feel very guilty sometimes. I am not a buttana. I was raised to be a good woman. I have only known my husband and you so…"

"Enough, Maria. Our love should have no guilt," Todò interrupted.

"I don't feel guilty of my feelings for you. I just think of my three children and your three children, you know, the new baby, and your wife, and I feel badly," Maria blurted.

Maria had never told Todò of Aspanu slaving in the mine. Her pride wouldn't let her. She admitted only to the three young children that Todò saw, when on occasion he stopped at her house for coffee.

Once Todò squeezed some lire into Maria's bosom. She threw the paper money in his face, proclaiming she was not a prostitute even though she could hear her children's stomachs growling from hunger at night.

A few times during his coffee visits, Todò would leave a few lire in a tin can in Maria's kitchen where she had kept some money. Maria questioned him each time there was more lire in the can, but Todò would deny it was he who left it.

One romantic evening in their special hideaway, Todò said, "My dear Maria, I am just happy that you brought your son to see Doctor Giordano that day. You know? I have never been to his office before or since. It was our destiny that we met at that moment. But please, let me help you a little. I…."

"Todò, no! Is that what you think of me? Money for…this?" Maria pointed to her lower parts.

"Not at all. But I know how difficult things are here, and I will not see you suffer so badly when I have more than enough. Now, I will insist that you allow me to bring you some food for you and your children," Todò blurted.

Todò, food, money, clothing...they are all the same to me. It is all charity, and I will not take it from you," Maria pronounced.

"I am a man of honor, and this is not honorable. I am not your husband, but you will respect my wishes. No one will ever know about us nor about the bread I bring to your door. My word is final," Todò insisted.

Maria brought her lips to her lover's lips and kissed him passionately. Todò could taste the salty tears as they ran down Maria's cheeks. They made love again that morning for the second time.

The apartment in which they shared their passionate lovemaking was very small, with only one room which had a small bed. There was a tiny kitchen area, a chest of draws and a crucifix on every wall. A wooden statue of St. Anthony of Padua had several sets of rosary beads around the saint's neck. Fresh posies were in a small glass next to the statue, and three, small, votive candles which were held in red, glass containers, were lit.

CHAPTER 33

The economy of Sicily had boomed until the late 1800s, due to the cache of sulfur which ran below most of the island. The economy boomed only for the mine owners, the men who made their living selling the product, those that transported the product and the gabbelloto, who were the mine managers, and of course, the government who taxed the product. There was no boom for the workers.

A piccionere made today's equivalent of sixty-cents per day, a basic subsistence level of income. These miners worked twelve to sixteen hours a day, simply for them and their families to be able to eat. The miners were forced to buy food at the bettolino, a canteen owned by the mines, at exorbitant prices.

The carusi earned mere pennies a day for their abject misery.

In the world of sulfur mining, there is surface mining like what had made Sicily the major source of sulfur for the world. The other source of sulfur was discovered in the United States. While digging for oil, sulfur was found deep below ground in Louisiana in the 1860s.

Lake Charles, Louisiana was the site where a large sulfur deposit was found while oil exploration was underway. The crude oil exploration was abandoned for the much more profitable sulfur.

Economics being what they were at the time, it was less expensive and more logistically feasible to mine the sulfur and ship it to the major world-wide users of the product from Louisiana than it was from Sicily.

By 1893, the death rattle for the Sicilian economy and the thousands of people who barely supported their meager existence, was near its final stages.

As if their torment wasn't bad enough, things got far worse for the carusi and the picconiere.

CHAPTER 34

The winter wind gave the surfataru a modicum of relief from the blaring, Sicilian sun. The gabbelloto took the cooler weather and the reprieve from the torrid heat as a reason to step up production.

Demand for Sicilian sulfur was on the wane by December 1893, and Lercara Friddi, as with many other Sicilian towns, had seen a tremendous amount of its families seeking immigration to the United States.

It was near the final whistle of the day Aspanu and Carlo, broken down with exhaustion from the now one hundred and twenty pound baskets of earth they carried, dragged their frail bodies like they were wet blankets.

The two carusi walked slowly away from the calcaroni and the sight of Nina, their mutual fantasy sweetheart.

"I guess one more load from below before that damn whistle blows?" Aspanu asked his friend. The reluctance in his voice was not lost on his friend.

"One more trip down there may kill us both. I'm sure Signore Alia is chipping away at the walls," Carlo replied.

"Let's just go piano, piano, slowly, and pray we hear that sound," Aspanu mused.

The boys moved slowly toward the vucca, imagining the relief they would get from the shrill sound of the mine whistle.

Suddenly, they heard a horrible, gravel voiced scream from behind them.

"Figghi de buttana. You sons of whores. Do you think you can pull this shit on me?" Signore Modica bellowed.

The squat gabbelloto was on top of the two boys before they could react. They couldn't run if they wanted to.

Modica slashed his barber belt across Aspanu's back with such force his basket went flying in one direction and his cap in another. Aspanu fell to the dusty ground, instinctively covering his face and head before three other whacks came down hard on his thin body. The boy screamed with every contact.

"You bastards! I've been watching you all day from the office window. I should have beat you like the dogs you are when you first got here. Now you will know my strap!" Modica screamed.

The gabbelloto, his eyes showing the fire of his wrath, turned on Carlo, who knew his turn was next.

The barber strap came across his back, whipping Carlo onto his stomach with such force Carlo lost his breath. The carusu could feel the skin on his back split open as he screamed for mercy. Carlo tried to use his basket to protect himself which enraged Modica even more. Modica whipped the poor boy three, four, five times more as Carlo hugged the ground. After the third time he was hit, the boy stopped yelling in pain.

"Now get the hell down into that mine and make three more trips. Tonight, the whistle is not for you two pigs," Modica shouted.

The gabbelloto walked back up to his office, wiping blood from his belt. He was satisfied with his brutality as other carusi scampered to and from the calcaroni. The pressure from the mine owners had made Modica worse than ever. As the demand for Sicilian sulfur dropped, the owners increased their demands for efficiency on the gabbelloto.

Aspanu and Carlo, weeping from the beating, scampered for their baskets and nearly crawled to the mine entrance.

"He deserves to die a thousand deaths," Carlo seethed through his tears.

Aspanu could not respond as he still struggled for breath.

The boys reached their piccionere, their faces streamed with dust and clotted with tears.

"Madonna mia! What the hell happened to you?   My God in heaven, you are both bleeding," Alia wailed.

"That devil beat us for moving slowly," Carlo whimpered.

Alia dropped his pick axe and tended to his carusi.

"How many times have I told you both to be careful and watch out for him?" Alia implored.

"I should stab him in his throat and take off into the hills like Turo did when he killed Dolce. I'd laugh as he choked on his own blood," Carlo pronounced.

"Nonsense. Don't even talk like that. These walls have ears," Alia warned.

"He told us to do three more loads," Aspanu said. He had just started to breathe again.

"Then you must. That animal will be watching, and he will kill you both if you disobey him. There is plenty of rock piled here. Finish the job, and I will take you both home. I promised your mamas I would watch over you and never beat you. I'm afraid they will think I went against my word," Alia whispered.

The three loads took almost two hours to complete. The badly beaten boys could see Modica, gazing from his office window, making sure their punishment was completed. Alia, with the bird cage in his hand, walked to the calcaroni after the third load was dumped. It was dark outside, and the mine property was abandoned.

"Let's go, I'll walk you to your homes," Alia commanded. He too was exhausted from his day of breaking down the mine walls.

"Signore. We will be fine. We will explain to our Mamas what happened, and that you had nothing at all to do with beating us. Go home to your wife and family," Aspanu replied.

Aspanu's logic made sense, and was a relief to the spent miner. Tears had welled in Alia's eyes as he turned from the boys and headed home.

"That miserable bastard Modica. I hope he chokes on his supper and spits blood before he croaks," Carlo pronounced.

"If I knew how, I would put a curse on him and his entire family," Aspanu blurted.

"One day, he will get what's coming to him," Carlo replied.

The two, shattered boys walked slowly back toward their homes, each of them saying how Modica should meet his end. As they approached the center of town, there was a small, lone figure standing in the shadows.

It was Nina.

CHAPTER 35

Aspanu and Carlo approached Nina as she came out of the darkness. Aspanu closed his eyes, then rubbed them, thinking he was seeing things. Carlo gave Nina a wide smile, as if he was expecting to see her. The boys stopped in their tracks, half believing that it was really Nina.

Nina was wearing a poorly-fitting cloth coat and a knitted hat which covered her ears. Her hair was pulled back into the hat. She was carrying a small basket.

"Ciao, Nina," Carlo offered.

"I saw what happened to both of you at the mine tonight. I felt so badly that I began to cry. I brought these wet linens for you," Nina responded.

Nina took two, damp towels from the basket, handing one to each boy. She had two, small, green apples. She handed the fruit, one to each boy.

"That is so kind of you, Nina. It's just what we needed," Aspanu blurted. He bit into the apple; the crunchy sound echoed against the doorway of a small building where they stood.

"If my Mama knew I was here, she would kill me with a kitchen knife. I sneaked out of the house. Mama thought I was sleeping."

Carlo kept staring at Nina's pretty face as he dabbed the cloth on his neck and head. He caressed the apple like it was a gift from heaven.

Aspanu wiped his face clean, thinking Nina did her act of kindness for him, and Carlo was given a cloth just so he wouldn't be embarrassed. Aspanu had a vivid imagination.

"How will you get back into your house, Nina?" Aspanu asked.

"Through the back door. I just hope the dogs in the yard don't bark. That would be the end of me!"

"Don't worry, the dogs will know it's you, and they will come wagging their tails," Carlo assured.

"Why did the gabbelloto hit you both? What did you do?"

"We were walking back to the vucca slowly. We were waiting for the whistle to blow so we could finally end the day," Aspanu answered.

"How is it working down in the mine? I would be very afraid," Nina asked.

"It's no place for a girl. It's usually very hot, and there is very little air to breathe. The smells are bad. I wish we didn't have to be there," Carlo replied.

Nina noticed both boys were scratching their sides as they stood talking with her. She couldn't imagine what that was about, but she said nothing.

"Nina, I have a question, if you don't mind?" Carlo asked.

"Sure?"

"How old are you, Nina?"

"Eleven. If the fumes from the calcaroni don't kill me, perhaps I will see my twelfth year."

"And if the mine doesn't blow up or collapse, we will see our sixth year, but only God knows that," Carlo blurted.

Aspanu was annoyed by his friend's forwardness. Who was he to ask such a question? Aspanu thought.

"Sometimes I would wish the mine would fall on some of those older carusi. Then I know you two are down there and I say a prayer to Santa Barbara that this will never happen. Those boys say so many bad things to me," Nina lamented.

"They are older than we are and have no respect for anyone," Aspanu commented.

"I wonder if someone spoke to their sister or mother like they speak to me, if they would even care?" Nina questioned. The thought of those ruffians brought tears to her eyes.

"You just let me know which ones disrespect you, Nina, and I will take care of them," Carlo bragged.

"And taste the belt again? Are you crazy, Carlo?" Aspanu asked.

Carlo began to retort as Nina interrupted.

"There is no sense to talk like that. I will ignore them as I always do," Nina declared.

"Very smart of you," Aspanu replied. Nina's wide, white smile made Aspanu forget the welts gabbelloto Modica placed on his frail body.

Suddenly, the sound of footsteps hitting the cobblestones came from around the corner, startling the trio. Nina gasped as Comandante Greco turned the corner with five of his carabinieri. Greco's men, dressed in their full uniforms, feathered hats, and polished, black boots turned the corner. In their midst was a man with his wrists bound with heavy handcuffs. Two of the carabinieri held their prisoner by either arm. The man held his head down low, his hat almost covering his face as he was marched toward the carabinieri office. Walking in front of the men with the Comandante was another man, dressed in a three-piece, dark suit wearing a top hat. Greco and the man were engrossed in conversation.

Nina, Aspanu, and Carlo ducked into a darkened doorway, out of sight of the men and their prisoner.

"I recognize that man," Nina whispered.

"I have to go now. Good night," Nina made quick steps toward the direction of her home.

"Wait, Nina!" Aspanu called to her. "Let us at least walk you back home," Aspanu said.

"Please, no. I will see you both tomorrow at the calcaroni. Six in the morning comes very fast."

"But, wait. Who is the man you recognized? Tell us!" Carlo asked.

Nina stopped walking, turned around quickly, and addressed the two carusi.

"When I went to school, there was a man who worked there. I knew his daughter. She was a bit older than me and very nice. Her name was Nina also."

"What is the man's name, Nina?" Aspanu pressed.

"That was Signore Lentini. The custodian for the school. Now, go!" Nina answered.

CHAPTER 36

Pietro Lentini sat in a stiff-backed, wooden chair in the cold musty basement of the Lercara Friddi carabinieri headquarters. His arms were tied behind his back with metal handcuffs, a thick rope attached from his copious torso to the chair. Both of Lentini's legs were tied to the front chair legs with a rough, brown twine.

Lentini was hatless, his necktie had been removed, and the candles which lit the basement made his eyes squint. The prisoner was sweating profusely, even though the room was cold enough to see the steam coming from the mouths of the other men in the room. There was no other furniture in the interrogation area.

The carabinieri who had tied Lentini to the chair stood close. They waited patiently for their superiors' arrival to question the frightened prisoner.

Comandante Greco waited for thirty minutes before entering the interrogation area, to build up anxiety in his detainee.

Greco walked slowly down the creaky, basement stairs in order to build added anticipation into his prisoner. Lentini heard the footsteps of two people descending into the underground room. The school janitor's eyes were bloodshot and bulging with fear. His eyes were uncontrollably darting from side to side.

"Mr. Lentini, do you know who I am?" Greco asked.

"Yes, signore. You are Comandante Greco," Lentini acknowledged.

Greco pointed to the man in the suit who was at Lentini's home when he was arrested.

"Do you know who this man is, Pietro?" Greco queried.

"No, signore," Lentini stated, his voice quivering.

"This is Signore Giuseppe Sorce. He is the Vice Prefect of the entire Province of Palermo Pietro. He and I will be asking you some important questions tonight. Depending on your answers and your cooperation with us, you may be able to go back to your family tonight. If you do not cooperate, you will be tried in the morning and likely be imprisoned by the state for a very long time," Greco stated.

"But Comandante, I've done nothing wrong. I have no idea why I've been arrested," Lentini stated.

"We shall see, Pietro," Greco replied. The Comandante looked at the Vice Prefect and smiled.

"Signore Lentini, tell me, have you ever heard of the Fasci Siciliani?" Sorce asked. The Vice Prefect, a tall, thin man who wore wire-rimmed glasses and a salt and pepper handlebar moustache, walked slowly around the chair which held Lentini. Lentini's blood ran cold when Sorce was behind him and out of his sight.

"Only what I have read on the notices and what I have heard in the taverns, Signore," Lentini lied.

"So, tell me what you've heard at the taverns, Signore," Sorce responded.

"What I've heard? I...I don't understand?"

Sorce kept his intimidating, slow walk around Lentini as he asked his questions.

"What is the Fasci all about, Pietro?" Sorce said from directly behind the prisoner.

"They want to change the conditions in the mines and on the farms."

"Correct!" Sorce shouted. Lentini nearly jumped out of his skin at the sudden scream from the Vice Prefect.

"And tell me, Signore, how do they intend to change things?"

"I don't know, Signore. I'm just a school custodian. I am not political," Lentini stated. Beads of sweat that formed on his forehead were making their way down into his eyes.

"Ah, yes...that reminds me. The school custodian. Well, Signore Pietro Lentini...we have been informed that you have allowed the local Fascio to meet on occasion, after hours at the school," Sorce stated.

Lentini tried not to swallow hard, but his bulging Adam's apple gave him away.

"Never! Never! I never let the Fascio meet at the school," Lentini blurted. The smell of the prisoner's expelled gas permeated the room.

Sorce gave a glance to Greco who nodded his head to one of the carabinieri. The officer pulled back on his black, leather gloves as he walked in front of the tightly-fastened Lentini.

Without a word, the policeman grabbed Lentini by the hair with one hand and slapped him hard across the face. Lentini felt like his head nearly snapped off his shoulders. The ringing in his ears made the Prefects next question almost impossible to hear.

"Maybe you didn't understand my question, Pietro. Let me try again, please," Sorce hissed.

Comandante Greco lowered his head for a second. Beating suspects was not his forte. Especially treating Lentini, a man he knew from around town, made Greco cringe. The whole political war between the mine owners and the Fasci Siciliani and the government made Greco's stomach turn. Greco's job, and for that matter, his entire career, was at stake. He could not show sympathy for an accused Fascio sympathizer.

"Please, Signore! I am a simple man. I know very little of these things," Lentini pleaded.

"Then tell me what we already know to be the truth, or this will be the longest night of your life," Sorce commanded.

Greco stepped forward.

"Pietro, I have known you for a very long time. You are a good man who maybe got involved with the wrong people. These Fasci are all insurrectionists, communists, who are not well regarded in Rome and Palermo. Save yourself from this and tell us the names of the men that have used you for their bad intentions," Greco advised.

"But Comandante, I have my family to worry about, my life will be nothing now, it…"

Before Lentini could finish his thought, Sorce gave another of the carabinieri a nod. A burly man, this policeman punched Lentini hard, square in his solar plexus.

The breath was pushed from the custodian's lungs, forcing his eyes to bulge from their sockets. He sucked in air to stay conscious.

Greco turned so as not to see the brutality.

Another of the carabinieri smashed a rubber hose to the back of Lentini's neck, causing the poor man to drop his head into his chest in a natural reaction to avoid another whack.

"Now that I have your attention, Lentini, tell me who you have allowed to use municipal property to plot against the government," Sorce shouted.

"I thought it was only a meeting to discuss the union. I am innocent of insurrection, my God, please…I…"

"You stupid man. I have the authority to take you into the courtyard and have you shot for what you have done. Wise up! I want the names of all the people who were in that school basement, now! Otherwise, you will be executed tonight," Sorce blurted.

"Will I have a chance to go to before a judge?" Lentini asked. He was barely able to speak.

"Signore Lentini, I am the judge, the executioner, and Jesus Christ Almighty. My patience is growing thin with you. I have others to interrogate on this matter. They will surely talk, so save yourself. This is my final offer!"

Lentini lowered his head. He took a huge gulp of air into his lungs.

"It was Francesco Piazza. I know him from when I was a child, but now he is the leader of this Fascio," Lentini answered.

"Now you insult me by telling me what I already know," Sorce yelled. A quick glance commanded the third carabinieri to punch Lentini directly on his face, splitting the custodians nose open. Blood ran from Lentini's nose into his mouth.

"Don't worry, Pietro, there will be no more beating. The next thing you will feel are the bullets which will smash into your body," Sorce chuckled.

Bernardino Verro and two of his men came from Corleone. From Lercara, there was Salvatore Panepinto, Luigi Romano, and Pietro Miceli, from the Mangiacarne group of Miceli clan. Lentini was choking on his own blood.

"Verro is very well known to us. So, for three names you want me to spare your life? I need more names," Sorce hissed.

The beating stopped as Lentini added seven more names. One of the carabinieri wrote the names onto a small piece of paper.

"Now, Signore, one more piece of information before I allow you to sit in a cell for a while. I need to know what they are planning. Your life depends upon this answer, my friend," Sorce demanded.

Lentini rolled his eyes to the ceiling. He looked at Greco for some sign of solace. There was none.

"A demonstration of workers here in Lercara Friddi," Lentini blurted.

"Ah, I see. And when will that be?" Sorce asked. He brought his face within inches of the beaten man. His beady eyes studied Lentini's face.

"Christmas day," Lentini lowered his head and sobbed.

CHAPTER 37

Aspanu and Carlo, beaten and bruised by the brutal gabbelloto, were soaked in their bagnera, a big bucket, and pampered by their mothers, both of whom wished a curse on Signore Modica.

The boys weren't at all concerned about their banged-up bodies. After all, Nina had come to see them. That meant the world to the two carusi. They both dreamed of her that night.

On the walk to the mine the following morning, Aspanu and Carlo's pace was rapid. The faster they got to work, the sooner they would see their Nina.

From out of nowhere, Carlo broke the silence.

"She is very beautiful!" Carlo said this as if Aspanu wasn't even there walking with him.

"Who?" Aspanu asked.

"Nina…of course. She is an angel."

"Yes, my angel," Aspanu declared. His smile was so big Carlo thought he looked like a raving idiot.

Both boys walked with their shoulders back and their chests pumped up, unlike their normal, slouched carriage.

"Are you crazy? Nina came to see me and you happened to be there," Carlo blurted.

"You are the crazy one, my friend. She was looking at me the whole time."

"The sulfur has gotten into your brain."

"You will see from her smile to me today. That smile!" Aspanu assured his jealous friend.

Some of the people in Lercara Friddi were preparing for the Christmas celebration. Others, the sulfur mine workers and the peasant sharecropper farmers, were getting ready for the Fasci Siciliani demonstration. The word was going around, through invitation via whispers, that the rally against the land and mine owners would take place in the town square, right outside Santa Maria Della Neve.

There would be no special feast for Christmas, except for the elite families who lived in the better neighborhoods of town. Those lucky few would have roast meats, baked goose, plenty of vegetables, and macaroni with sausages, finished with copious homemade desserts, and of course, delicious and abundant wine. Among the working class, food was so scarce most of the population looked gaunt and pale. Some of the young children had distended stomachs from starvation.

Because of the heavy taxes, which took away the possibility to have a few extra lire, Christmas day would be much like any other day for the workers who broke their backs for the owners. The laborers prayed with their families the Fasci Siciliani would overcome the government and the gluttonous titleholders.

Christmas day fell on Monday, so the only good thing this day brought to the peasants was not the celebration of the birth of Jesus, but a much-needed two days off from the drudge of work.

The day after the Vice Prefect had beaten and frightened information about the Fasci Siciliani out of Pietro Lentini, Sorce went to see Monsignor Paci at Santa Maria Della Neve.

There was a young couple in the monsignor's office in the rectory. It was Domenico Alia and his wife, Rosalia. Rosalia, who was dressed in the traditional, black mourning dress and veil, was weeping inconsolably. Alia had the gray look of a mine worker with his large hands, stooped back, and broad shoulders.

"My dear. The angels came because it was God's will. We cannot question His plan. Remember a few years ago when one of your children was near death with influenza? We prayed together and a mass was said for the child. God answered all of our prayers and pulled the boy back from death. That was also God's will."

The woman continued to wail so loudly Sorce considered waiting in front of the rectory for the couple to leave.

He looked at his pocket watch, annoyed this nuisance was interrupting his official visit to speak with the monsignor.

"Now," said the Monsignor, "go home and pray and prepare for the child's funeral. Domenico, take your wife back home and then go to work. There is nothing you can do for your family by mourning. Leave the prayers to your wife while you do your job as a man to provide food for the table. And Signora Alia, pray for your dearly departed. Right now, your rosary is the best thing to help see you through this time."

"Thank you, Monsignor. We are grateful for your words," Domenico Alia said meekly. The piccionere spoke only a little above a whisper. The miner fiddled with his workman's cap the entire time.

"Now, both of you kneel so I can give you my blessing," Paci stated.

After the blessing, Domenico helped the forlorn Rosalia to get up from the kneeling position. Alia walked his still sobbing wife from the rectory, his arm around her waist, holding her up.

Paci called after them, "I assure you, this Christmas, your son will be playing with baby Jesus in heaven. And remember… you are both young enough to have another child if it is God's will," Paci imparted to the young couple like it was an afterthought.

Rosalia and Alia's fourth born child, Giorgio, had succumbed to pneumonia at only four months of age.

"It is good the baby was christened so his soul is already in heaven and not purgatory," Paci declared, his voice trailing off as he heard the rectory door close.

As Domenico and Rosalia passed the Vice Prefect, Domenico made quick eye contact with Sorce. A quaking shiver went down the picconiere's spine he had never felt before in his entire life.

Aspanu and Carlo both smiled at Nina as they approached the mine property entrance. Nina could only smile with her eyes because Signore Modica was nearby counting the carusi as they entered the mine property. The light from the torches at the calcaroni reflected off of Nina's face, giving her an angelic glow. Soon the sun would rise, the torches would be extinguished, and Nina's pretty face would be clear on the boys first drop off.

"You two bastards. Get over here now!" Modica yelled. The gabbelloto pointed at Aspanu and Carlo who ran at his command.

"Let me catch you dogging the job again, and you will wish you were never born. Now get your asses down the shaft like lighting. By the way, your picconierie will be late today. One of his kids croaked last night. Use the small picks to break some ore off the walls, you weak dogs. I want to see your baskets full. Now, go, you sons of bitches."

The boys ran for the vucca and the safety of the mine in order to put distance between themselves and the devil Modica. When they got under cover, the boys stopped and looked at each other with fear and sadness in their eyes.

"Mischinu, that poor thing, Signore Alia. That sick baby finally passed on," Aspanu lamented.

"What can we say to him?" Carlo asked.

"I don't know what to say," Aspanu replied.

"Sorry? That sound so stupid," Carlo blurted.

"Let's just make as much rock as we can and carry it to the bin so when he gets here, at least he will know we care about him and we feel badly for him," Aspanu reasoned.

"This life is bad enough then his baby goes and dies," Carlo said.

"Maybe the baby was destined for a life like ours. Maybe he is better off in heaven," Aspanu mused.

"You really are an idiot, Aspanu. I'm going to call you Babbu from now on," Carlo announced.

"And when you see me walking with Nina when we are older, holding her hand, you will refer to me as Signore Salerno, dottore Salerno, professore Salerno...."

"Vaffanculo Salerno," Carlo corrected.

CHAPTER 38

Salvatore Todaro knocked softly on the door at 25 Via Cimò. He listened at the door to hear if anyone was home. The mafioso carried a burlap bag which was slung over his shoulder.

Maria Salerno opened the door and smiled at her lover. She looked around to see if anyone was watching or peeking from the windows from the houses next to or across from her house. Seeing no one, she beckoned for Todò to enter.

The couple embraced and kissed passionately.

"Tongues will be wagging in this entire town if anyone sees you coming here," Maria spouted.

"And if my name is mentioned they will be making a big mistake with their lives. Don't worry, my love, no one was watching. I made sure of that," Todò replied.

"The children are all at school so we have some time together. Can I make you some coffee, Todò?

"That is about all the time I have today. I have to see someone on this side of town. Near the mines. The boss asked me to drop an envelope for a couple who just lost a baby. He is a sucker for sad stories. Do you know the name Alia? He is a miner, maybe he worked with your husband," Todò queried.

Maria felt her blood run cold. Maybe this was the time to tell her lover about Aspanu and her guilt at taking the soccorso di morti from Signore Alia.

"I learned of the baby dying from the washerwomen in town. They say the father is a good man. He has other children, I think," Maria lied. Her shame prevented her from exposing the truth about her oldest son. Maria had fallen in love with Todò and didn't want to risk losing him. *Perhaps another time,* Maria thought.

"Make the coffee hot. I don't suppose you have any anisette?" Todò asked.

"I happen to have some homemade anisette that my late husband made. I have not opened it since..." Maria stopped in mid-sentence.

"Good, that will be his gift to me. Here, I have some things for you and your family."

Todò lifted the bag onto the kitchen table. He lifted a small, dark, twisted cigar to his lips, took out a stick match, ran it under his shoe and lit the stogie.

"My God, Todò! What have you brought?" Maria asked with concern. She didn't feel comfortable accepting charity, even from her lover.

"That is for you to discover, my love. But pour me the coffee so I can watch your face."

Maria busied herself at the stove, her fingers trembling in anticipation of going through Todò's bag.

A few minutes later, Maria poured a large cup of black coffee as Todò struggled to chip off the sugar which encased the top of the anisette bottle. Once opened, the gangster poured a shot of the clear liquor into his coffee.

Maria blessed herself before digging into the burlap sack.

"You look like a little girl opening a Christmas present, Maria," Todò remarked.

A large package wrapped in brown butcher paper with a bit of dried blood was the first of the items to be taken from the bag. Maria unwrapped the gift and gasped.

"It's beef! My God, I can't remember the last time we..."

"Look into the bag. There are fresh potatoes that you will roast with the meat. That will feed your kids for a few days," Todò offered.

"But...but where did you get this gigantic roast, Todò?

"Where else do you get meat? In a pharmacy? In a butcher shop, Maria," Todò laughed.

"It must have cost a fortune!" Maria declared.

"It's nothing. The butcher owed me a favor, and I thought of you.

"Look at these plucked chickens and these fresh eggs. My goodness, I...I..."

"Roast, fry, make soup, prepare it any way you like, Maria," Todò offered. He was beaming with delight at Maria's excitement.

Maria began pulling out package after package from the sack, announcing what was in the bag one item at a time.

"Fresh ricotta, and look, a bottle of olive oil, and...oh my, a jar of marmalade. Todò, we haven't ever seen this much food on this table."

Maria kept trying to find the bottom of the sack.

"And...Madonna, shoes for me? Look how beautiful they are, Todò! I have to try them!"

Maria threw off her worn slippers and replaced them with the elegant, tan, dress shoes that were in the bag.

"They fit perfectly! I've never had shoes like this in my entire life. When will I ever wear them?" Maria asked.

"One day I will take you to the Politeama theatre in Palermo," Todò announced.

"Palermo? I've...I've never been to Palermo. And what if we are seen together?"

"So then we are seen."

"And your wife, Todò She will be furious, and my name will be like dirt in this town."

"Stop worrying. If you are with me, everything will be fine. Just trust me."

Maria moved into Todò and kissed his passionately again. The mafioso knew if they got started, it would take a long time. He hugged Maria and gently moved her away from him. Her passion for him was something he had never experienced.

"Todò, most of the people of this town are near starving, and I am blessed that you have come into my life and the lives of my children," Maria whispered. The widow began to cry.

"I hope they are tears of joy, my love," Todò said.

"Of course. But what of these poor men and boys that work in the fields or in the mines?" Maria thought of Aspanu again, her heart pounding in her chest. She wanted to tell his story to her lover but could not find the words. *Soon, very soon I will tell him,* Maria thought.

"That is not our concern. Let the Fasci fight for them. Those socialists will all be sent to jail or shot, then things will go on as they always have. In my borgata, my family, we work with the people who have money. In my world, the rich respect us, we look out for each other. They make money and we make money, that is all you need to know, Maria."

"I understand my place, my love. Tell me more of Palermo and the theatre, Todò."

CHAPTER 39

Domenico Alia dragged himself to the mine after having settled his sobbing wife at home.

Alia pushed his worn body to work every day, but this day was different. As he crept along the dusty streets of Lercara, all he could see in front of him was the face of his dead baby boy. The child was always smiling and was making baby talk noises. The infant would kick his feet wildly with excitement whenever he saw his Papà, making the evenings enjoyable to everyone in the house. The sound of his wife's sobbing and wailing rang non-stop inside Alia's ears and brain. It was nearly too much for the picconiere to bear.

When he arrived at the vucca, Aspanu and Carlo were coming out of the mine carrying their third load of the day to the smoking calcaroni.

"Signore Alia, Aspanu and me have been chipping away, low on the wall you were working on. This is our third load of the day," Carlo bragged.

"We knew you would be late today, so we did our best for you," Aspanu added.

"Good," Alia muttered. That was all he was able to say. His spirit was broken.

When the boys got to the calcaroni, Nina could sense there was a problem just by the look on their faces.

"What's wrong?" Nina mouthed.

"Our picconiere, his little baby died," Carlo said into his hand. The boys were looking in all directions for gabbelloto Modica. If he caught them talking openly to Nina, they would taste his belt again.

"Oh, God!" Nina mouthed again. She then blessed herself with the sign of the cross, kissing her hand and offering it up to heaven.

Aspanu lifted his basket, dropping it into the bin, Carlo did the same. Both boys offered their sad eyes to Nina, who was wiping tears from her eyes.

Hustling back to the mine, the two carusi friends moved quickly down the shaft, returning to Signore Alia.

Alia, smashing his pick axe harder and faster than ever before, was sobbing, his tears streaking his sulfur-dusted face.

Aspanu looked at Carlo, and both boys began to gather rock for their baskets. The boys didn't know what to say, so they worked as the rocks fell onto their heads and backs.

"What is this life but misery!" Alia exploded.

"Signore Alia, what can we do?" Aspanu asked.

Alia ignored the question.

"You work until your bones hurt, until your blood hurts. You suck in this devil's gold, never seeing the light of day, never seeing your children at play. Work until you drop, and still, the babies are hungry. For sinful wages! Never enough to eat or save a few lire for the future. What will I do? Die in this stinking pit of Satan. And the priest tells us to pray. Pray for what? Pray to whom? A God who never listens? A God who punishes us for our thoughts, our past sins? A God who gives diseases to babies and little boys? And, if He decides to crush us beneath these rocks or blow our bodies to pieces in an explosion, and we are buried here until our bones rot, who will care?"

Alia's, pick axe was moving in every direction, smashing into every wall in their section of the mine. Aspanu and Carlo began to cry from fear their picconiere would die of heart failure right in front of them. Little did they realize that if Alia died their soccorso di morti would be cancelled and they would be free from their indentured servitude.

"I piss on God, I piss on all the saints, I wipe my ass with the pictures of the crucified Jesus, I condemn Santa Barbara to the fires of hell," Alia lamented. His chest was heaving with every strike of the gray rock while yellow streaks of sulfur ore poured out all over his torso from perspiration.

Finally exhausted, Alia fell into a heap, his naked body heaving up and down as he tried to suck in the little oxygen the mine floor offered. His sobbing and screaming stopped as suddenly as it started.

Aspanu reached for the picconiere's pick axe, sliding it from under his perspired body and placing it against a darkened far wall.

The boys quickly filled their baskets, lifted them onto their stooped, bruised shoulders, heading as quickly as they could to the surface.

"See what I'm saying to you, Aspanu? Do you now understand what a pathetic life we are made to live? Do you see now what the Fasci are trying to do for us?" Carlo whispered.

"Shut your mouth, stupid idiot. And if someone hears you, we will both be sent to prison, or worse," Aspanu whispered in response.

"When the demonstration comes, I will be in the front of the crowd, throwing rocks at the pig owners. I may be a stupid idiot but I am no coward like you," Carlo seethed.

"I feel sorry for you, Carlo. This is the life that we have to lead for our Mamas and our brothers and sisters. You are no good to them dead."

"I would rather be dead than a weakling who is afraid to stand for what is right."

CHAPTER 40

Aspanu and Carlo weren't speaking to each other by the end of the day. Never mentioning Signore Alia had his melt-down inside the mine.

They finished the day hauling their filled baskets to the calcaroni without a word while walking a good distance from one another. For the past four years, they marched their loads, walking no more than three yards from each other, sometimes Aspanu taking the lead, sometimes Carlo walked ahead. Very often they walked side by side before they dumped the rocks into their bin.

After they argued, the boys were ten to twenty yards from each other. None of the other carusi noticed this change in Aspanu and Carlo's routine. The other carusi had their own problems with which to to deal. Treacherous picconieri who would mistreat them, beat and whip them, and even sodomize them on occasion, was more than any child should have to bear. Cuts on their feet from sharp rocks, infected scabs on their hands and knees from slipping and falling, the hookworm that invaded their malnourished bodies and their lack of proper nutrition made the carusi no more than pack mules to the mine owners and gabbelloto.

The only person who noticed the boys had estranged themselves from one another was Nina.

By the end of the day, even when Nina glanced or smiled in their direction, the boys seemed to be in a state of remorse, not even noticing their mutual crush.

When the whistle blew, and Signore Alia walked Beppe and his bird cage out of the mine, Aspanu and Carlo headed back home, dejected and apart for the first time since they started working in the mine.

Nina waited until Aspanu and Carlo left the mine before she left her station at the calcaroni. She was usually able to leave a few minutes before the carusi, but today her curiosity got the better of her.

The boys were just not themselves as Nina approached. They walked on either side of the street, practically ignoring her. Their boyish smiles toward the girl were gone, replaced by a dull, defeated stare. Nina walked down the middle of the dusty, dirt road, put both of her hands on her hips and waited for the boys to walk toward her. Other carusi were walking home as well, some of them made cat calls, while others, the older boys, made unpleasant remarks. Nina ignored them as if they didn't exist.

"What's wrong with you two?" Nina asked.

Both Aspanu and Carlo stood looking at the ground. Carlo kicked the dirt.

One of the carusi let out a whistle and announced, "Look, Nina has a babysitting job. If she needs a man, I volunteer."

Carlo made a move toward the older boy, but Nina grabbed his arm, holding him in place.

"Okay, this is no place to talk. I will see you around eight o'clock in the same place we met before," Nina announced.

The trio walked away from one another as though they were strangers.

◇◇◇

Just after eight o'clock that night, Nina arrived to where she had waited for them once before. Aspanu and Carlo were waiting, staying clear of each other, not talking.

"Sooner or later, my Mama will realize I'm out of the house at night, and the wooden spoon will be on me. If she finds out I'm meeting boys, she will send me to the convent in Catania," Nina said.

"I would rather be in Catania shoveling horse dung than doing this work," Carlo blurted. Aspanu remained silent.

"What's wrong with you two? How can you be friends one minute and angry the next? What happened?"

Carlo glanced at Aspanu hoping he would talk first.

"We have been friends since the cradle. We lost our Papàs on the same day in that unholy mine. The next thing we knew, we were slaving away for pennies. Carlo wants to join the Fasci Siciliani, and I think they are not so good. It's simple, we can no longer be friends," Aspanu stated.

"You would rather be led like a sheep to slaughter than stand up together with the Fasci and make all of our lives better. The union will help us against the owners," Carlo blurted.

"This is what you believe, Carlo. I don't believe that. The Fasci are criminals to the government, and they will be shot in the streets or sent to prison. Is that helping?" Aspanu replied.

"You are a fool…"

Nina interrupted Carlo.

"Now stop this bickering like two dogs in the street. Can I ask you both a serious question? Can I?"

Both boys nodded.

"Can either of you read?" Nina asked.

Carlo and Aspanu looked at each other quizzically then looked away, each remembering their feud.

"Well? Can either of you boys read?"

"Read? No, of course not. I only went to school a short while and then the mines," Carlo answered. Nina looked at Aspanu for his reply.

"No, I never learned to read or write. Maybe one day," Aspanu mused.

"How can you not read and make an argument about politics? You are both boys who will remain below the ground until you are old men without learning to read and write," Nina preached.

"How are we supposed to read when we are in the mine all day, every day except Sunday?" Carlo asked.

"Can you read, Nina?" Aspanu said.

"Of course I can read. I learned a little about letters at school, and then I needed to work, but I kept trying and trying, asking anyone that I knew who could read and write to help me. I still get stuck on large words, but then I ask and I find the answer. My father's friend, the barber, Signore Cangelosi, helps me all the time. He taught all his children to read and write. I can teach you both," Nina offered.

The boys instantly forgot their war of wills. The thought of learning to read and being with Nina was an offer they had to take.

"But where? But when?" Carlo asked.

"We will have to make time. I say we start right after the Christmas celebration. Maybe I will ask my Mama if you can come to our home a few nights or on Sunday afternoon to learn. As long as she and my aunts are around, it will be acceptable," Nina offered.

"Fine by me!" Aspanu blurted.

"Me too!" Carlo added.

"Okay then. There will be no more arguments between you two about the Fasci or anything else. I will teach you both to read. After all, you will not be working in that silly mine forever. And when you boys stop working there, you will at least be able to know your letters and get a better job. Maybe even go back to school…who knows?"

"Can we start tonight?" Carlo asked. He was always more impetuous than Aspanu.

"I have to get home before Mama finds out I'm not sewing or sleeping. So…after Christmas we begin!"

CHAPTER 41

Vice Prefect Sorce sent a telegram to General Roberto Morra di Laviano who had encamped himself and his large militia on the outskirts of Marineo. Military intelligence, using local resident spies and mafiosi, informed the general that Marineo, Lercara Friddi, and Belmonte Mezzagno were the likely towns where the Fasci Siciliani were plotting large demonstrations by disgruntled workers. Word had by now spread throughout the province eleven peasants were killed and twelve were wounded in the town of Giardinello at a Fasci uprising. The Fasci Siciliani had demanded an abolition of food taxes. Nothing would change.

"ARRESTED ONE PIETRO LENTINI STOP TESTIMONY LED TO APPREHENSION OF FASCIO LEADERS FRANCESCO PIAZZA, SALVATORE PANEPINTO, LUIGI ROMANO, PIETRO MICELI STOP COMM GRECO GIVING FULL COOPERATION STOP CHRISTMAS DAY PLANNED RALLY LERCARA. STOP CORLEONE LEADER BERNARDINO VERRO AT LARGE STOP"

Morra was aware of Verro as a former Mafiosi associate and Fasci insurrectionist. The general had issued orders to the carabinieri comandante in Corleone to arrest Verro on sight. If Verro resisted, he was to be shot.

Sorce and Greco spent their time interrogating and torturing Panepinto, Romano, and Miceli to gather more names of Fascio sympathizers. Their brutal tactics led to another dozen arrests. The carabinieri jail in Lercara Friddi was at capacity, and the school where Lentini was custodian was now closed and commandeered for more prisoners of the state.

Doctor Alfonso Giordano went to the Church of Santa Maria Della Neve to see Monsignor Paci. The nearly depleted physician was at his wit's end. He interrupted the prelate's lunch.

"Ah, Dottore! This is a wonderful and welcome surprise. Maria, put dishes down for Doctor Giordano, he will join me for lunch," Paci ordered. The housekeeper moved quickly to fulfill the monsignor's command.

"Monsignor, thank you, but I have no time to eat. Actually, no time and no stomach. My visit is of great importance," Giordano said. The tone of the doctor's voice was urgent.

"This roast lamb is delectable, and the macaroni is without peer. Just a small taste? Or a nice glass of Barolo, perhaps?"

"So as not to be rude, I will take a coffee while you eat, Monsignor."

The housekeeper scampered to the kitchen for the doctor's coffee and fresh-baked biscotti.

"What brings you here, old friend? You look tired and worn," Paci inquired.

"I'm afraid there will soon be uncontrolled violence in our town, Monsignor. The workers are telling me there will be a large demonstration, one of all times, Christmas day, here in Lercara."

"I see. So why are you not telling this to Comandante Greco or the Vice Prefect? What does this have to do with me and the church?" Paci responded.

"The police and government, I am sure, are aware of the rally. I am afraid that there will be a similar outcome that occurred in Giardinello. Too many killed or wounded, Monsignor."

"Are you certain you've had lunch? This lamb and these vegetables are heavenly," Paci blurted. He was not interested in hearing any more from the doctor.

Giordano stood up from his chair and pointed at the sumptuous display of food.

"Just look at you! You are eating like a sultan while there is impending violence on the steps of the church. My God, can't you speak to the parishioners and ask them to stand down? Aren't there enough people dying here from malnutrition and disease in this town?"

"Alfonso, you should mind your tongue in this place. After all, we are on church grounds. I am not going to interfere with the business dealings of the mine owners and land owners. We have been down this road before and you know very well what my position is and what my superiors have ordered."

"This is not business, Monsignor, this is wholesale slaughter. The workers have rocks and sticks against rifles and swords. It is bad enough the mines have become cemeteries. Why does blood have to run in our streets?" Giordano pleaded.

"And what shall I say? Ignore the Fasci Siciliani and their socialist union teaching? Ignore Karl Marx who said that religion is a poison? These are rebels in suits and neckties. The church has no responsibility in this regard," Paci seethed.

"Certainly, your church has a moral responsibility to prevent murder."

"The government in Rome has determined these insurrectionists are a danger and detriment to the Italian economy. I must remain with the teachings of Christ. Matthew tells us that Jesus said, 'render to Caesar the things that are Caesar's; and to God the things that are God's,'" Paci quoted.

"Yes, I recall. And Luke quotes Jesus, too, 'Let the little children come to me, and do not hinder them, for the kingdom of God belongs to such as these,'" Giordano responded.

Paci finally put his fork down. His face reddened in anger.

"Do not dare use the words of our Lord to preach political insurrection, Alfonso. That is sacrilege."

"Jesus himself was an insurrectionist in his time. Today, the Lord would be considered a socialist, Monsignor," Giordano countered.

"You wear on my patience. This conversation is finished. Please do not end our friendship on a bad note. I will not hear the name of the Lord taken in vain."

Giordano left his coffee untouched. The great doctor and scientist unceremoniously walked out of the rectory dining room.

Monsignor Paci, his face still scarlet, resumed eating his lunch.

CHAPTER 42

It was a chilly, Christmas Eve Day in Lercara Friddi, a Sunday when the mines were closed and the field workers and the braccianti, the laborers, prepared for Christmas day.

For the peasants and mine workers, the Christmas eve dinner consisted of a small piece of baccala, dried, salted codfish made into a casserole. With the fish, some macaroni and vegetables, bread, and a sweet cassata dessert. If they even had that. Some had nothing to eat at all.

Some of the workers, although they labored like slaves, went hungry for the day. The blaring recession in Italy and Sicily had turned the country into near collapse, a condition of which the Fasci Siciliani was taking full advantage.

The workers in Lercara Friddi were thrilled to have a rare two days off. The townspeople were electrified with talk of the Fascio's plan for a mass demonstration on Christmas day.

Mayor Sartorio and the Nicolosi family were hard at it, fighting for control of the town both politically and economically. The mayor made sure printed copies of a letter he had sent to Prime Minister Crispi, with Crispi's response, were handed out and posted throughout Lercara Friddi. Although not many of the workers could read, there was always someone who would read the contents of the correspondence to small groups of people.

Sartorio's letter asked for Crispi and his administration in Rome to intervene and settle the tax and land issues. Crispi responded with promises to make changes, but warned the workers should avoid instigators who were out for their own gain. This was a shot across the bow of the Fasci Siciliani.

Aspanu and Carlo were enthused with the possibility of seeing Nina at the evening mass and possibly sitting close enough to smile at her and hear her sing Christmas hymns. Carlo was particularly energized by the rally scheduled for the next day. Aspanu was indifferent about the workers demonstration.   The carusu had a gnawing felling of impending doom.

"Tonight will be a great night, Aspanu. My Nina will be at mass and I will see her in a beautiful dress, and tomorrow I will be at my first Fascio march. You will see how things change after tomorrow, my friend," Carlo preached.

"You say 'my Nina' like you are her picciottu. She is not your girlfriend, and you are just saying that to make me angry. I know your silly game and you are stupid. And Carlo, I wish you would forget this Fascio meeting, if it even happens. I have a very bad feeling about the whole thing," Aspanu advised.

"That's because you see your future bent over like so many smelly old men we see in the mines every day. You can stay down there for all I care. I will not be a carusu very much longer, because I refuse to spend the rest of my life crawling underground. You will see," Carlo bragged.

"And you will disobey the carabinieri warnings not to participate in the demonstration? And you will risk your life for strangers who will use you just like the rest of the world is using you? Just like a slave!" Aspanu challenged.

"What do you know? Soon Nina will teach me to read and write, and I will become someone famous in the Fasci. My name will be in the newspapers all over Sicily and Italy, maybe even around the whole world," Carlo dreamed aloud.

"Idiot, Nina said she will be teaching us both to read and write. I'm much smarter than you, and Nina will pick me as her husband one day. You can go play with your union and find a wife somewhere else," Aspanu stated.

"I've had enough of you. I am going to a meeting now to discuss tomorrow's rally. I have men's work to do. Maybe I'll see you at the church tonight unless I'm needed with the Fascio leaders," Carlo crowed.

"Yes, and I am needed by the Pope in Rome to help him with his Christmas mass!" Aspanu mocked.

Having just lost their infant child, there was no cause for celebration in the Domenico Alia household.

Rosalia tried her best to overcome her sadness, but the loss of her little, baby boy was just too much for her to bear. When she wasn't crying, rosary in hand, she was sleeping, rosary still in hand. Her other children remained quiet. They felt their mother's pain and their own sense of loss for their cute, baby brother.

With the death of his son, Alia turned bitter toward his faith and government. His already cynical attitude toward the mine owners and the gabbelloto had turned hostile.

Suddenly, Domenico Alia was determined to be part of the planned protest which was gaining wide attention and momentum among the workers in town. Alia left his grieving wife and children to listen in on some of the Fascio leaders in a clandestine meeting at a farmhouse near the sulfur mines.

When Alia arrived at the farmhouse, owned by the family of Luigi Romano, one of the men who were jailed by Comandante Greco and Vice Prefect Sorce, he was amazed at all of the familiar faces he saw who were sympathetic to the Fasci Siciliani and their cause.

One familiar face stood out and shocked the piccionere Alia.

"Madonna mia! Carlo! But ...what are you doing in this place? You are only a kid!" Alia blurted.

"Signore Alia, Buon Natale! Merry Christmas to you. I'm here to support the Fascio and do what needs to be done to make our lives better," Carlo quipped.

"This is no place for a carusu. If you are caught, I will lose a worker I paid for, and you will go to jail," Alia whispered.

"And if you are caught, you will be jailed, and I lose my job, and I'm free to do whatever I want to do," Carlo reasoned.

"Hmmm, you are smarter than you look, Carlo."

"And you are braver than I thought, Signore Alia."

The meeting didn't last very long. The workers were gathered in the presence of Fascio leaders including Francesco Piazza and other leaders, along with several, very vocal, women sympathizers.

The small crowd at the Romano farmhouse was revved up for the next day's demonstration which would amass in the town square. Piazza gave an impassioned plea to pass the word to any and all workers who wanted the tax levies to be removed and working conditions for farmworkers, miners and the carusi to be improved. Piazza began to cry when he spoke about five-year-old boys being used in the mines as carusi. He demanded changes to prevent such atrocities.

"From those blood suckers, Gardner and Rose, to the current low life mine owners, our children have lost their youth I curse the rich of Lercara. I curse the devil's gold which has made rich men richer and these poor children enslaved without hope," Piazza declared. He pointed directly at Carlo whose shaved head looked too big for his frail body.

"Little boy, how old are you now?" Piazza asked.

"I will have ten years soon, signore," Carlo replied.

"And when did you begin working in that mine?"

"I was five years old, Signore. My father was killed in the sulfur mine owned by Gardner-Rose, and I had to go to work."

Piazza put his hand to his mouth, dramatically stifling his trembling lips.

"A baby! Five years old! This must stop! I am willing to die for this cause rather than live with the shame of these children, and others who will come after them, suffering through their childhood for these bastards," Piazza erupted.

All of the workers, about forty-five of them who jammed into the house, raised their arms in solidarity and screamed their approval of Piazza's challenge.

The meeting ended, sending the workers to gather their friends and Fasci partisans to prepare for the largest demonstration ever seen in Lercara Friddi, perhaps in the whole of Sicily for that matter.

The zeal these men and women had after Piazza's impassioned speech took a startling turn that afternoon.

A crowd gathered within the town and in spite of the carabinieri warnings to disburse and clear the streets, the group decided to ransack and burn the toll houses which were set up to collect that tax levy.

The word of the riot traveled as fast as the smoke from the burning toll houses as it waffled through the entire town.

Mayor Giulio Sartorio, seeing what was going on in town on the eve of Christmas and hearing from his friends and associates a dangerous mass demonstration was being planned for Christmas day, decided to take bold action. He believed this action would win him favor with the moneyed elite in Lercara and votes in the next mayoral election.

Sartorio by-passed Vice Prefect Sorce and wrote an urgent telegram directly to General Morra, and the Prefect who never shirked from their responsibilities to intervene against any Fasci Siciliani rally. Morra had developed a taste for executing Fasci leaders and sympathizers and having his men gun down peasant protesters.

Sartorio called for troops to be sent forthwith to quell the planned Fascio demonstration. He implored General Morra to move as quickly as possible to save the town from ruin.

"We are all in danger, and I am not exaggerating," Sartorio wrote.

The General immediately dispatched a company of militia to Lercara Friddi, who he himself would accompany.

Morra also ordered four battalions of regular army to be sent from Naples to Palermo.

The Fasci Siciliani dei lavoratori would, no doubt, be taught a lesson in Lercara Friddi.

CHAPTER 43

Aspanu had a meeting of his own to attend. It wasn't actually a meeting, per se. Aspanu had a sneaky idea in his head from the time Carlo said he was going to the Fascio meeting.

While Carlo was listening to the forbidden rants of the union leaders, and risking his freedom, Aspanu went to where Nina lived to see if he could at least get a glimpse of his infatuation.

The carusu must have walked past Nina's house a dozen times hoping to catch sight of Nina. Maybe she would sweep the front steps, or perhaps feed the chickens, or wash a window, something to grab Nina's eye that he was on her street.

Aspanu could hear Signora Miceli singing a Christmas song, her voice carrying from inside the home, filling the tight alleyway with a melodious, festive sound.

Suddenly, as luck would have it, Nina walked out of the front door just as Aspanu passed again. The boy pretended not to see her.

"Aspanu? Is that you?" Nina called out.

"Yes…oh, Nina! Buon Natale! I didn't realize you lived here," Aspanu fibbed.

"My whole life. I was born in this place. I will probably die here."

"Don't talk like that. I can't think of you dying," Aspanu blurted. The carusu felt silly saying that, but the words were already out of his mouth.

"Walk with me to the store. Mama sent me to get a few things before they close," Nina offered.

"And will you get in trouble walking with a boy?"

"Don't worry, I told Mama and my aunts all about you and Carlo and how I will teach you both to read and write after Christmas. Mama thinks it's very sweet, and she said you can come to our home whenever we can steal time for the lessons. Where is Carlo?" Nina asked.

"I...I don't really know, Nina. He said he had something to do," another fib by Aspanu.

They walked toward Via Garibaldi where people were bustling around from store to store to gather last minute goods in preparation of Christmas.

"I am so happy to see you, Nina. Can I confess something?" Aspanu asked. He could not look at the taller, young woman, keeping his gaze to the cobblestones below.

"Of course you can, but I cannot absolve you of your sins like at church," Nina answered. Her reply caused her to giggle.

Aspanu had no idea what absolve meant. He had not yet taken his confirmation. Signora Salerno wanted nothing to do with the church, especially after Aspanu's father was killed in the mine explosion. If the church would not have a funeral mass for her husband, she would only say her prayers in private, and even that was not sincere any longer.

The carusu paused, thinking of the right words to use. He didn't want to embarrass Nina or himself. Mostly himself.

"Well, I...I think you are very beautiful, Nina. You are the prettiest girl in all of Lercara," Aspanu uttered. His voice was low and he felt the heat rise up into his face.

"How sweet of you to say that, Aspanu. That may be the nicest thing a boy has ever said to me."

Nina stopped walking and looked at the starry-eyed boy.

Aspanu finally looked into Nina's eyes. They were more beautiful than he remembered. Her smile brought a tingle to him he had never felt before.

"But I...I am only... a carusu who..." Aspanu began.

Nina interrupted the stammering boy. "Aspanu! You are a carusu now! One day, after you learn to read and write, you will never have to say only again."

With that said, Aspanu was now even more in love with Nina.

They walked on, talking about their two days off from work and how they both needed the peace and quiet away from the loud machinery and a reprieve from the smell and smoke of the cooked sulfur ore.

"Christmas is not the same without my Papà," Nina declared.

"Nothing in my life is the same since my Papà was..." Aspanu said. He could feel a cry coming on, but he wouldn't dare shed a tear in front of Nina.

"My Mama said that all the men who lost their lives in the mines were murdered by the mine owners. Do you think that's true, Aspanu?"

"I never thought of it like that."

"I thought it was their fate. I put my trust in God. He must have needed their souls for His reasons that we will never understand."

"I don't think about God. I just think about getting through each day, and seeing the morning come again and suffering through whatever happens."

"But if you ask for God's help, maybe your prayers will be answered," Nina offered.

"How do you pray? With the rosary? I know some of the words but sometimes I get mixed up and stop," Aspanu replied.

"You can just ask for God to change your life, make it better somehow. I use my own words. I ask God to keep Mama and my sister healthy. I pray that the mine doesn't collapse or explode. So far, since my Papà died, my prayers have been answered."

Nina went into the general store for a few items her Mama needed. Aspanu waited outside. He was beyond gleeful Nina was being so nice to him. The carusu thought he was in a dream.

Nina and Aspanu walked slowly back to her home. Aspanu carried the small package for the girl. They talked about a hundred things. It never dawned on Nina that Aspanu was so smitten by her. To her, Aspanu was just a nice boy who didn't deserve the life he was forced to lead in the mines.

Aspanu didn't want the time with Nina to end but she had to go back inside her home to help her Mama. Nina politely took the package from Aspanu.

"Are you going to the mass tonight, Aspanu?"

"I think so, yes."

"Maybe I will see you there. If not, I know Mama wants to see the demonstration of the workers tomorrow in front of the church. Perhaps I will see you then. But we all have to be careful. Mama said we will not stay too near the crowd. There could be trouble," Nina stated. Nina moved quickly into her house, but not before she waved a goodbye to Aspanu before finally closing the door.

Aspanu ran the entire way back to Via Cimò. The cool, early evening breeze rolled over the carusu's cap, his eyes watering from the dust in the air.

He hadn't felt this happy and free in quite a while.

CHAPTER 44

Maria Salerno visited her lover at their usual hideaway. She planned the afternoon so she would have time with Salvatore Todarò and be back at her home before dark. Her mother and aunt were with the children, preparing their delicious and plentiful dinner, courtesy of the Mafioso Todò.

Later that evening, Todò would be at the home of his cousin, Benedetto Di Prima, for a sumptuous Christmas Eve dinner with his wife and children.

Votive candles in the small apartment gave a soft radiance to the two lover's afterglow.

"Maria, you are the most beautiful woman I've ever known," Todò whispered.

"And you are the most handsome man in the whole world."

The light shining into your eyes almost takes my breath away. I wish our worlds could be different."

Maria's head was resting softly on Todò's chest. The candle light reflected bits of green in his large brown eyes. She averted her eyes and looked away so their eyes no longer met.

"I love you, Todò." Maria said. She could not bear to look at him, fearing her words would perhaps be met with an unkind glare.

"Love is a very strong word, Maria. To me, it's like a contract. It binds people together. I'm afraid to use that word," Todò responded.

"Have you ever told your wife you love her?" Maria asked. She still could not look at her lover's face.

"We were an arranged marriage. She was promised to me by her father to my father. It was a marriage of two families in my world. I love her as the mother of my children, that is all I can say. Did you love your husband, Maria?"

"For the same reason as you, yes, I did love him, but the struggles we had overwhelmed us. I never said I loved him. It was a difficult marriage, but I was forced to know my place. You are the only man I said these words to."

"And you know your place now, as well?"

"Yes. I know what I am in your life."

"And you are willing to live this way?" Todò whispered.

"Until the day I die...yes, I am," Maria sighed.

She finally looked up at Todò again with a glimmering smile. *Is this the moment I tell him of Aspanu?* Maria thought. The idea was fleeting.

"I must tell you something you will not repeat," Todò stated. His mood became somber.

"I give you my word."

"Tomorrow there will be serious trouble in Lercara. I don't want you to be in the center of town with your children," Todò warned.

"What kind of trouble? Because of the burnings today?"

"Yes. There are militia coming to meet the demonstrators. The owners of the farms and mines control the carabinieri and the military. We play both sides, but in the end, we follow the money."

"So, nothing will change?" Maria asked.

"Nothing!"

"But the union seems very strong. They have many followers."

"The owners are stronger. Money is more powerful than a gang of workers. Money puts bullets into the guns of soldiers. This is always the way things have gone in this world," Todò stated. He kissed Maria's forehead gently.

"Will you be safe, my love?"

"I will be sipping coffee out of the way of danger. And you will be at your house, I insist."

"Of course. As you wish."

Maria returned to her home, the foreign smell of roasted meat and the sight of her pots filled with vegetables and macaroni brought her eyes happy tears. Her mother and aunt gave knowing looks, the kind that needed no words.

The older women made the traditional dessert in the wood fired oven in the small house. Li cuccidati was a round type of donut with chopped, dried figs, toasted almonds, and pieces of chocolate, all courtesy of Todò.

Aspanu was playing a game of knucklebones on the floor with his siblings.

"Aspanu, are you teaching them the same way that your Papà had taught you?"

"Yes, Mama, but this little one only knows how to throw the bones all over the room."

"It reminds me of you at that age," Maria declared. She giggled at the memory of another time.

"Where were you, Mama? I thought you would be home all day," Aspanu asked.

"I went to the church to light some candles for Papà and other relatives. It's an old family tradition," Maria lied.

Maria's mother looked at her sister. Both women rolled their eyes in silent comment.

"Aspanu, tomorrow I want you to stay at home with all of us. There are things that may happen in town that you are better off avoiding," Maria spouted.

"But Mama, I cannot stay here. I want to be with some friends for Christmas."

"This Christmas will bring danger and sorrow. Best you stay here, I said."

"I have a day off and I must be treated like a baby? What if I told you I'm meeting a girl?'

"A girl? Aspanu, you have no need for girls. What do you care about girls?"

"It's not just a girl. This girl promised to teach me to read and write so I might become more than a mere carusu."

"And who is this girl teacher of yours?" Maria demanded.

"Her name is Nina and she works at the mines. She is a nice girl, and I like her," Aspanu replied.

Aspanu's nonna said something he didn't understand. Her sister laughed while almost dropping a platter of food.

"Mama, please!" Maria barked.

"You will have plenty of time for girls and to learn how to read and write another day. For tomorrow, we are all staying here, together," Maria commanded.

"You said I was the man of the house. Am I only good for work?"

"You are the man of the house, but you are still my son and a son must obey his Mama."

"And tonight? I want to go to the mass!" Aspanu replied.

"Maria, it has the strength of twenty horses," Maria's mother stated. She pointed to her own crotch.

"Mama, enough!" Maria yelled.

"Suddenly you care about church? Will that girl be there?" Maria questioned.

"I was planning to go with Carlo. I like the singing," Aspanu fibbed.

"Fine. Then you come directly home after mass, understood? And you will stay home tomorrow?

"Yes, Mama," Aspanu blurted. The carusu put both of his hands behind his back, crossing his fingers for the lie he just told his Mama.

CHAPTER 45

Santa Maria Della Neve church was filled to capacity for Christmas Eve mass.

Monsignor Paci and two of his priests were preparing to say the high mass in celebration of the birth of Jesus Christ.

To the right side of the main altar, in front of the sacristy was a presepe, a nativity scene that had been handmade in the 1700s by the original parishioners of the church.

Wooden hand carved figures of the virgin Mary, her husband Joseph, shepherds and their farm animals, the Magi and their camels, angels, donkeys, and oxen were displayed in a cave-like setting, replete with rocks taken from the sulfur mines.

All that was missing before the mass was the infant Jesus in his cradle. During the mass on Christmas day, a small procession of nuns and church elders and children laid the infant in his straw, mattress crib in a dramatic recreation of the Lord's birth.

After the peasants and workers had all taken their seats, Mayor Sartorio and his family walked boldly down the aisle to take the reserved seats in the front row. The Mayor made sure he was seen by many. He shook hands or waved to the most important people in town, including his rival Nicolosi and his wife. The political and personal disdain these men felt toward each other took a temporary reprieve for the sake of the faithful.

Behind the opposing politicians sat Bernardino Di Prima and Salvatore Todaro and their families.

In the row behind the mafiosi sat Comandante Greco and his wife and grown children, with Greco's grandchildren, wide-eyed with excitement.

Doctor Alfonso Giordano sat alone in a chair behind Greco and his family. The town's physician looked worn and tired, his shoulders hunched over with concern for the many sick people in the church who he had been treating.

Standing aside the baptismal font, at the rear of the church, were the captains of the carabinieri, their keen eyes fixed on the entrance to the church in case any Fasci Siciliani leaders were bold enough to attend the mass. They would have been immediately arrested. There was no sanctuary in the church for wanted men.

Near the rear sat Nina, her sister, and Signora Miceli and her aging mother and aunts. There were no men left in this family, all victims of mine accidents or disease.

Aspanu and Carlo pushed their way into the seats two rows behind their friend Nina. Other carusi attended the celebration with their families. The carusi dotted the crowd of faithful with their shaved heads and gray pallor, a memento of the shame of Lercara.

Every woman, the beads entwined in their hands, said their silent rosary during the mass.

Nina wore a dotted blue and gray sweater and black skirt, her head covered with a small, lace kerchief. She sat erect, taller than her family, her hair flowing onto her shoulders. Nina looked around the church, studying the paintings and statues that depicted the lives of Jesus, Mary, and the saints.

Aspanu and Carlo studied Nina.

Carlo nudged Aspanu and nodded his head toward Nina. "Look how beautiful she is," Carlo whispered. Carlo smiled broadly showing how proud he was of 'his' friend.

"We're in church. Show some respect," Aspanu answered.

"This will be the place that I marry her one day. After tomorrow, she will see what a man I am and become proud of me," Carlo blurted.

"She will have to visit you in jail, you fool," Aspanu whispered.

An old woman, dressed in the black dress and veil of a widow, poked the boys in their backs, telling them to be quiet and listen to the mass.

Monsignor Paci's sermon followed the reading of Luke and his story of the birth of the savior. Paci spoke of the peace of embracing the Lord and contributing to the church. He said nothing about politics and the unrest that morning nor of the potential disaster which might follow the next day.

Carlo and Aspanu both fought hard to keep their eyes open, nodding out a few times as sleep called to them.

When the mass ended, the two carusi sat and waited for Nina to pass. When she saw them, Nina smiled politely in their direction. Her gracious recognition was an emotional reward for both Aspanu and Carlo.

That night was restless for many of the people of Lercara.

Monsignor Paci could not sleep the entire night. The words he had with Doctor Giordano were echoing in his mind. Paci was a good and true priest, who was caught up in the politics of his church. The monsignor knew there would be serious problems in the shadow of his church this Christmas day, and he was powerless to change it.

Maria Salerno fell asleep after quite some time of restless tossing and turning. She dreamt of making passionate love to her Todò in his own bed. She dreamt that Todò's wife found out about her relationship with Todò and left for America while leaving her children behind.

Mayor Sartorio, happy he shook so many hands and kissed so many voters on both cheeks, tossed and turned until he fell asleep just before dawn on Christmas morning. Sartorio was confident troops would be in Lercara to quell any demonstration the Fascio organized.

He was proud of his part in supporting and defending his own financial interests in the sulfur mines.

Comandante Greco reviewed his reports on the Fascio arrests until his eyes went blurry. Greco had called for all members of his carabinieri to be at the ready for any demonstration in the town center. In his mind, Greco worked out the positioning of his men around the church and within the square. His mind raced with possibilities and contingencies.

Aspanu slept restlessly. The excitement of walking and talking with Nina, then seeing her at mass, sent his senses reeling. The carusu made his decision during the night to disobey his Mama and go to the demonstration in the hopes of seeing Nina and perhaps meeting her family.

Salvatore Todaro fell into a semi-sleep. His mind was on Maria and her children. He knew she would listen to his warning to stay home rather than join the crowd of onlookers during the planned demonstration.

Vice Prefect Sorce stayed awake all night in a catatonic state. He stared at the church of Santa Maria Della Neve and the town square from his rented apartment.

Carlo, excited by what he imagined his role was to be in the demonstration and what the future would hold for him, stared at a statue of St. Francis of Assisi until he fell into a deep sleep.

In the morning, General Morra would march with his men to meet the Fasci Siciliani head on.

The general slept like a baby.

CHAPTER 46

At dawn on Christmas morning, a small band traveled throughout the town playing Christmas songs in front of the votive niches, all decorated with fragrant bay leaves. The music sounded the commemoration of the birth of Jesus.

Soon, the aroma of freshly baked bread and fried zeppoli filled the small streets and alleys of Lercara.

Aspanu and Carlo woke at five as usual. Carlo dressed, had his usual breakfast consisting of a cup of sheep's milk and some bread. Aspanu had some milk, a small piece of pecorino cheese, and some olives from the family tree.

At nine o'clock that morning, in spite of his mother's edict to remain at home, Aspanu snuck out of the back door of his home and headed for the town square. Carlo was sitting on the church steps when his friend arrived.

The carabinieri were already stationed at each of the four corners of the square. Two elderly widows in their mourning dresses walked through the large, green doors of the church to light candles for their dead husbands and other family members who had passed.

Nothing else had signaled potential trouble at that hour.

Without a word to his friend Aspanu, Carlo walked away from the square. Carlo walked quickly past a few uneasy-looking carabinieri, disappearing onto a side street.

The church bells tolled at ten o'clock. Ten, slow dings, and still no crowd had formed.

Vice Prefect Sorce and Mayor Sartorio arrived with Comandante Greco. The three men had their morning coffee at a small tavern at the far side of the square, facing Santa Maria Della Neve. They walked slowly across the empty square, waiting anxiously in front of the church.

Suddenly, the sound of a crowd in the distance could be heard.

The demonstrators, nearly one thousand or more, made their way toward the square, walking down the middle of the street leading to the town square. A chilly, December breeze blew directly into the faces of the marchers, some of them carrying sticks from olive trees and other vegetation which surrounded the town.

Alongside the marchers, walking on the paved sidewalks, were dozens of onlookers, old men, women and children, and other curious citizens. From other streets which led to the square, came more observers who wanted to witness the Fascio Siciliani and the workers who supported their movement for the mass demonstration.

At the front of the demonstrators was Francesco Piazza and other members of the Fascio. All of the leaders and organizers of the uprising were dressed in business suits, unlike the workers who wore their normal daily work attire. In the crowd of marchers were many women who also joined in the rally, mostly farm workers and widows of dead miners who came to honor their husbands.

Dozens of carusi, looking like starving waifs, dotted the crowd of protesters. Some were marching in solidarity with their picconieri, while others with clusters of young carusi who came to demand improvements to their hellish working conditions.

One young carusu, his cap pushed back on his shaved head, his left shoulder drooping well below his right, his arms looking too long for his body, walked at the front of the angry mob. It was Carlo Panepinto.

Aspanu was dumbfounded. Here, his best friend was doing exactly what he said he would do. Carlo said he would one day be someone important in the Fasci movement. He had said many times he would lead men and become an important part of the union. Carlo often boasted how he would help organize workers and get out of the mine, become an official in the union, marry Nina, and have the respect of everyone in town.

An impulse told Aspanu to run to his friend Carlo and drag him away from the crowd, which seemed to be growing quickly. As he began to make his move toward the crowd of protesters, he heard his name being called from across the crowd.

"ASPANU! ASPANU!"

It was Nina. There she was, bundled up in a heavy, wool jacket, waving a tattered scarf in the air to get Aspanu's attention from across the square. Nina was standing with her mother, aunts, and younger sister, all of them curious bystanders of the union march.

Aspanu paused for a moment, then began to run toward Nina, forgetting about his urge to confront Carlo.

"Aspanu, what is Carlo doing? Is he completely crazy?" Nina asked.

"He is right in front like he said he would be. If his Mama saw this, she would be screaming at him to get away," Aspanu blurted.

Nina's mother's attention was on the swelling crowd. Signora Miceli did not notice her daughter's familiarity with a boy. Under normal circumstances, Nina would have been admonished about her forwardness.

The sound of boots hitting the cobblestones in unison on the far side of the square unexpectedly added to the confusion of the moment. All eyes were on the uniformed soldiers who were wearing long rifles over their shoulders. The militia was led by a striking figure on horseback who wore a uniform with medals and ribbons, adorning his massive, erect chest. Several other officers were on horseback. Their horses were bobbing their heads or stomping a hoof, reacting to the noise from the crowd. The officers knew how to command the animals with a tug on their reins or a pat to their sweating necks.

General Morra tipped his cap to an officer who blew a whistle, commanding the men to halt their march. The officer bellowed an indistinguishable command. The men hurried in two lines to the top of the stairs which led to the entrance of the church. Two men broke ranks and ran to the side door of the church.

Upon seeing the soldiers line up in front of the crowd of demonstrators, the carabinieri quickly ordered anyone standing on the sidewalk to leave the square. Some obeyed the command, while some were frozen in disbelief the scene was taking place in their town, directly in front of the main church.

Francesco Piazza, reading from a prepared agenda, began bellowing out the list of items the Fascio were requesting. After each demand, the crowd roared their approval.

Aspanu was frozen with fear. He and Nina watched their friend Carlo as he and others in front of the demonstration began taunting the soldiers.

With each stipulation from Piazza, the crowd boomed, becoming more and more agitated.

From the windows and balconies in the affluent homes along the square, the residents, mostly the wealthy gentry affiliated with the mine and land owners, shouted down at the crowd. The residents sent obscene gestures to the throng of workers, along with chanting their feelings.

"Death to the instigators! Death to the Fascio!"

This enraged the assembly to the point the demonstrators couldn't hear what Piazza and the other Fascio leaders were shouting.

The workers started their own chant.

"Down with taxes! Down with the Mayor!"

Feeling that discretion was the better part of valor, Comandante Greco sent two of his men with Mayor Sartorio into the safety of the church.

Vice Prefect Sorce saw the crowd was becoming unruly. Sorce hastily entered the town hall building and addressed the throng from the second-floor balcony.

"Please! Please! This crowd must stay calm. I will see to it that the new taxes are abolished. On my word, I will make sure your voices are heard. This demonstration must disburse. For the safety of all, please return to your homes. In a few day's time the taxes will be ended," Sorce screamed.

The crowd wanted no part of the Vice Prefect, who they looked upon as a brutal lackey of the government. His words were not even heard by most of the horde.

Sorce repeated his promise to no avail. Rocks began pinging off the building and balcony where Sorce stood with two other town officials. The men retreated into the building, fleeing the building from a back entrance. Sorce's life was clearly in danger.

The crowd's fuse was lit by the wealthy spectators from the balconies around the square as well as the sight of Vice Prefect Sorce.

The demonstrators began hurling rocks and sticks at the troops in a desperate sign of civil disobedience.

Aspanu and Nina watched in horror as Carlo was throwing rocks at the soldiers at a maniacal pace. Carlo's face seemed to be twisted in anger, while he was biting his lower lip.

As the crowd surged forward, the militia stood at attention awaiting their orders. The workers finally crossed the point of no return as the mob began ascending the steps in front of the soldiers.

General Morra raised his sword with his right hand. With his left hand, he was attempting to steady his black and brown stallion. The steed bucked and turned in semi-circles.

Some of the carabinieri stationed around the square took cover behind buildings along with some of the onlookers; others took to safety behind the troops.

The General bellowed out his first command.

"Guns at the ready!"

CHAPTER 47

Nina grabbed onto Aspanu's hand in anticipation that something dreadful was about to happen.

Many of the onlookers on the sidewalks began to flee for safety while others stood frozen in absolute disbelief.

The demonstrators lunged forward, their rants undecipherable. They were now no longer a union rally but an angry mob.

The next two orders to the soldiers came in rapid succession. There was no order to fire warning shots.

"Aim! Fire!"

A hail of rifle bullets blasted into the crowd. A mist of blood shot into the air. The ranting from the crowd turned to screams of pain and disbelief.

The hardened soldiers, who had shot into civilian crowds before, in several towns in Sicily, placed their second bullet into their breech-loading rifles.

The two soldiers who had earlier entered the church from the side entrance had made their way into the bell tower. The snipers had taken their shots into the crowd, using the church building to shoot to kill the demonstrators.

The wounded and dead lay bleeding on the pavement in the town square. Women were screaming from the horror of what they had just seen as they ran in different directions toward the safety of their homes.

"Oh, my God, they are ready to shoot again!" someone yelled.

A second volley screamed into the disbursing crowd, felling even more demonstrators. One of the two snipers in the church bell tower aimed his rifle at a fleeing peasant, leading him perfectly and firing, splitting his head open like a melon.

The general ordered his men to stand down.

The screams from the wounded and those who ran to attend to them were blood curdling. Someone called to summon a priest, someone else hollered for a doctor. Someone cursed Jesus as a criminal for allowing this slaughter to occur.

"My God in heaven...Carlo!" Nina screamed.

As Nina and Aspanu ran toward their fallen carusu and friend Carlo, Signora Miceli screamed for Nina to come back to her. Nina couldn't hear her mother's voice from the wailing of the others around the square.

Carlo lay in a puddle of blood. A bullet had passed through his right side, exiting through his left. His eyes were glassy as he stared up to the sky.

"Carlo! Carlo can you hear me?" Aspanu pleaded.

For a few seconds, the boy did not respond. Carlo focused on Aspanu and then looked up at Nina.

"Aspanu...Nina. What happened to me?"

Nina began sobbing

"The soldiers shot into the crowd," Aspanu replied. Tears ran down his gaunt face.

"I feel nothing...but I cannot move," Carlo exclaimed. His eyes closed briefly. When they reopened he began to cry as he stared up again to the cloudy sky.

Aspanu raised his friends head into his lap, crying uncontrollably.

A whistle sounded from one of the military officers and the militia returned to attention, their rifles shouldered.

Doctor Giordano arrived at the scene. He began checking the pulses of the fallen workers. Some were obviously dead, others were writhing in pain on the bloody pavement.

Signora Miceli ran to her grieving daughter, pulling her away by her arm. Nina had no fight in her and left without a word.

Aspanu let the doctor and his assistant tend to Carlo. The assistant pushed Aspanu away, telling him to go home.

Twenty minutes had passed before the militia were commanded to walk single file from the square.

Monsignor Paci and two other priests appeared dressed in the vestments they had worn for mass, blessing the dead and wounded with small bottles of holy water.

The square was littered with dead and wounded. It looked like a battle scene. The carabinieri had called for a horse-drawn carriage to take the wounded to Giordano's clinic. The carabinieri, with the help of some of the demonstrators and bystanders, began carrying the wounded to the cart.

Aspanu could see the wife of Signore Alia kneeling next to her husband. The boy ran to his picconiere's side. Alia was gravely wounded with a wound to his chest. Aspanu became completely immobile from shock. Suddenly he felt someone tugging at his arm. It was Maria Salerno. She pulled her son to her chest, relieved he was uninjured.

"Mama, Carlo has been shot!"

"Come my son, this is no place for you. We are going home," Maria said through her tears.

Doctor Giordano, his suit covered with blood, stood erect in the square. He caught the eye of Monsignor Paci who was kneeling and praying beside a fallen woman worker. Paci could not bear to look at the doctor.

That evening a list of the known dead was placed around the town, no doubt circulated by the leaders of the defeated Fascio.

Antonino Di Gregorio, 32, farmer.

Gaspare Mavaro, 22, laborer.

Francesco Piazza, 50, bricklayer

Michele Siragusa, 55, mine worker

Stefano Vicari 32, no occupation

Maria Greco, 32, farmer

Teresa Seminerio, 26, farmer

Francesco Piazza, who was among the seven, reported killed, was the Fascio leader in Lercara. He was the first to fall and die from the shots fired by the militia. Piazza's death was a major blow to the Fascio. He insisted on having the demonstration in spite of the impassioned plea and warnings against a rally from Bernardino Verro, the Fascio leader in Corleone. Now, Piazza was dead and Verro was being sought by the authorities as an instigator of the unlawful assembly.

The list of those who were killed did not include Domenico Alia, although he had died at the clinic. Two days after Alia was shot dead, Doctor Giordano signed a false death certificate which stated Domenico Alia had died of natural causes.

Although at least four others had died in the square, they were deemed to have died of natural causes by Doctor Giordano so the church could have a mass and bury them with all Catholic honors. The others, those reported on the initial list, had died from violence and would not be brought into the church for a mass.

CHAPTER 48

The next day, the town was reeling in grief. Unnatural death came in many forms in Lercara Friddi but never from such violence as was seen on Christmas day.

Those who died in mine explosions, from sulfur gas, collapses, heat exhaustion in the mines and in the fields, and other industrial mishaps were a way of life. Being shot to death in front of Santa Maria Della Neve was too much for the citizenry to accept.

Many of the mine workers did not report to work, sending the gabbelloto Modica into a fit of rage. The mine owners demanded their quota each day, but this day, the volume which was required, simply was not going to happen. Most of the field workers abandoned the farms in an emotionally-driven boycott.

Mayor Sartorio, like any politician, was assessing his position as the town's leader and trying to gauge the damage to his reputation. His future as mayor was bleak.

Carpenters gathered the wood to assemble plain, pine coffins for the dead, many of the families could not afford the cost of the caskets.

Doctor Giordano, drained from all of the wounded he was attending, had sent word to physicians from neighboring towns to assist him with the wounded. The fear of a rising death toll through infection and loss of blood was prominent in Giordano's mind.

Elvira Panepinto spent the entire rest of Christmas day and into the next morning at the clinic with her son, Carlo. Doctor Giordano gave Elvira very unpleasant news. They met in the docto'rs cluttered office just after dawn.

"Signora, please listen to me carefully. Your son has been gravely injured. A bullet passed through his body and he is stable. However, it seems to me that his spinal column has likely been severed," Giordano began.

Elvira gasped. She blessed herself three times.

"I am asking for a doctor whom I know well, from Palermo, to come to Lercara to help me diagnose Carlo. We have no way of seeing into the body, and surgery of this kind, to repair the spine, is not possible. Sometimes the body can partially heal itself from this trauma, but it seems to me that your boy will be paralyzed for the rest of his life."

Elvira fainted dead away.

Elvira was taken to her home in a total state of shock. She was attended by friends, among them Maria Salerno, who sat by her side placing cool compresses on her forehead and wrists and pressing olive oil and garlic cloves to Elvira's temples.

Word had gotten to Maria Salerno that Domenico Alia was dead. Even though his name was not among those killed in the square, the news had been verified by someone who knew Alia and his young wife.

Aspanu and Carlo's soccorso di morti died with Domenico Alia.

Maria returned home to explain the news to Aspanu who never got out of bed that morning. The boy's stomach was aching all night.

"There is some brutal news, Aspanu. Two things I must tell you. Please sit here by Mama," Maria offered. She sat in an upright chair, handmade by her late husband. She beckoned her son to sit on her lap.

"Aspanu, beddu, my beautiful son. You never have to go to work in the mine again. You can now find work that is not so difficult," Maria whispered.

"But why, Mama? Because of the demonstration?"

"No, Aspanu, because God lifted his finger for you. Some are saddened by the news I will tell you, but you can be happy now, maybe even return to being a boy," Maria declared.

"I don't understand you, Mama," Aspanu blurted. He was confused by his mother's around-a-bout words.

"You see, you are free because Signore Alia is dead. He died yesterday from wounds he received at the square. Your hard life may still be hard but you will no longer be suffering in that cursed mine."

"Dead? Like he is really dead?"

"Yes, he is dead."

"And what about his family? His little sons? How will they manage?" Aspanu queried.

"This is indeed very sad, but not your business, Aspanu. Perhaps his wife's family will help them. We must worry about you now," Maria replied.

"What if you need me to go back into the mine to put some food on the table for our family like we did before?"

"Things have changed a bit lately. I have a friend to talk with that may have a solution for us."

Aspanu gave his Mama a puzzled look. He waited for the second piece of news.

"I came from Signora Panepinto just now. The news about Carlo is very unhappy," Maria said.

"How is he, Mama? Will he be…"

"He is paralyzed. He may never be able to walk again. I am sorry to be the one to tell you this."

Aspanu pale face turned scarlet with anger.

"I told him! I told him never to get involved with those communists. Now his dreams are over, his life is over. He is not even good enough to be a low carusu. How many times did we argue about this. I almost punched his face once. Now…now he is like a…." Aspanu burst into tears. Maria held him close to her breasts while rocking him back and forth like she did when he was a baby. After a while, Aspanu looked at his mother with the saddest face she had ever seen.

"Mama…in one day, Signore Alia is dead, my best friend Carlo is crippled, lying on his back like a vegetable, and I am free. The only bit of joy in that mine was seeing the little bird Beppe each day. He will be the only thing I will miss."

CHAPTER 49

Maria took a chance and went to the social club where Benedetto Di Prima and his men of honor played cards and drank black coffee. Aspanu was at home, watching his siblings. He was still in a state of numbness over what his mother had told him.

Maria didn't dare walk into the storefront, as it was clear women were never allowed inside. She walked passed several times in the hope Todò would see her.

A few of the men noticed the pretty woman, but as men of honor, would not make a cat call or any other improper advance.

After her third pass, Todò came walking around the corner, nattily dressed in his suit and fedora, heading for the storefront. Todò saw Maria, and he immediately knew something was wrong.

"Maria? Is there a problem?" Todò asked.

Maria's heart melted when she saw her love. Her heart raced knowing that the conversation she was about to have with Todò could end their affair.

"Yes, Todò, something is wrong."

Todò asked her to follow him. He walked quickly down the street and into a tavern. Inside, there were several men sitting drinking coffee and other drinks. The owner was tending the bar. Todò gave them a stern look and motioned with his head for everyone to leave. The men, and the owner of the establishment, complied immediately to the mafioso's non-verbal command. They would see, hear, and say nothing as their lives depended upon their silence.

Todò waved Maria inside the bar, offering her a seat in a rear table. He sat across from her. His look was serious, showing no sign of his affection toward her.

"So, now tell me what is on your mind," Todò asked politely.

Maria swallowed hard, her heart pounding so hard that she could see her own blouse moving under her open jacket.

"Todò, I have not been totally honest with you, and for that I am deeply sorry," Maria whispered. Her lower lip trembled as if she was about to cry.

"Tell me," Todò said through his clenched teeth.

"I have another son. With my husband, of course. He will soon be six years. All the time I have been with you I wanted to tell about him but was ashamed," Maria blurted.

"Ashamed of your son? What is wrong with him?"

"He has worked in the mine for over four years. When his father died, I needed to put food on my table and sold him in a soccorso di morti, to a miner. The miner is a very good man. Todò, my son is a carusu. I am so humiliated," Maria confessed.

"A carusu?"

"Yes, he was until his piccionere died on the square from the soldiers. His name is Gaspare. We call him Aspanu. He has always been a good boy and has suffered greatly for his family." Maria suddenly felt warm all over, freed by her confession to Todò.

"You did what you had to do, my love. Your decision must have been very difficult," Todò declared.

"It was an impossible choice. And now that you came into my life, I am afraid to lose you because of my dishonesty."

Todò looked deeply into Maria's eyes. A grin appeared onto his chiseled face.

"My entire life is based on dishonesty. Why would I judge you for something that you were forced to do in these difficult times? Where is the boy now?" Todò asked.

"He is at home with the other children. He was at the demonstration and saw the workers killed right in front of him." Maria's lip quivered again.

"You said he suffered greatly?"

"As if working in the mine was not bad enough, a short while ago he and his best friend Carlo were beaten badly by the gabbelloto. Beaten so badly that Aspanu had welts all over his little body. Now Carlo has been crippled by a bullet from those horrible soldiers." Maria explained.

"What is this gabbelloto's name?" Todò's eyes looked darker than Maria had ever seen.

"Modica. I have cursed him every day since. To beat two boys like he did...an animal."

"And what will Aspanu do now?"

"I don't know. He is not well. His body is broken down from the work. He scratches his stomach constantly. He may have the hookworm but...I don't know what to do. I think the best thing for my son is to start a new life. Maybe like so many others from Lercara, he should go to America but this is not possible at the moment. Maybe someday."

"Have you told him this?" Todò inquired.

"No. Part of me wants him to remain here with me, of course, and part wants him to have a better life. I have Miceli cousins in New York who left three years ago. I am sure they would take him in and give him an opportunity to work and be safe," Maria said.

"Who are the relatives?"

"My cousin is Pietro Miceli. His wife is Dorotea Salerno. They have three children with them. No one has heard much from them since they left."

"I don't know of them. What did your cousin do here in Lercara?" Todò asked.

"He worked on a farm and did some labor work. They scrimped and saved. Pietro left a year before he sent for his family. There are other Micelis, all from the Mangiacarne group of the Miceli clan, who live in New York."

"You go back home to all of your children now. I will look into this thing for you. In a few days, I will tell you what I have discovered."

"And us?"

"What of us? Nothing can ever change between us, Maria. Nothing!"

CHAPTER 50

All of the miners and carusi returned to work at six o'clock the next morning. No one could afford missing another day's work for fear of losing their jobs and forfeiting the few lire needed to feed their hungry families.

A few of the returning picconieri huddled together to discuss the events of the Fascio, the soldiers and the recent wounded and the dead.

Giuseppe Modica scurried down the steps from the mine office near the calcaroni. Nina was at her position waiting for the carusi to bring their baskets to load into their bins.

Modica was screaming every obscenity imaginable at the miners who had not yet entered the vucca and into the mines, to pick away all day at the walls.

"Sons of whores. You damn dogs, standing around like wash women at a fountain. Get to work or I will smash your heads in for you," Modica barked. His arms were flailing in every direction as he spit onto the dusty, barren ground as an added insult to the men.

The carusi scampered into the mine so as not to taste Modica's wrath from his ever-present belt. The miners walked slowly to the mine entrance, their hearts filled with contempt for the hysterical gabbelloto.

Suddenly, three men appeared on the mine property. They walked toward Modica as if they were walking down the Via Garibaldi on a Sunday afternoon.

Modica turned to address the men. He never saw the first blow coming. One of the men punched Modica's face so hard, some of his teeth actually flew from his head. The gabbelloto fell to the ground, holding his swollen and bloody mouth.

All three of the burly men began kicking and stomping on Modica's stomach and barrel chest. One of the men kicked the downed gabbelloto's face until it was a bloated, blood-splattered mess.

The miners, all shocked into motionless, watched as the three men tore into Modica with silent vengeance. A few of the carusi watched the beating from the mine entrance.

One of the three men ripped the barber belt from Modica's side and proceeded to whip him to within an inch of his life. The gabbelloto's face was unrecognizable.

Finishing the incessant pounding, the man with the belt threw it on Modica's thrashed body.

The three associates walked away, never uttering a word.

When a mine owner arrived, the carabinieri were summoned.

The officer of the carabinieri questioned the miners, carusi, and even Nina and the calcaroni workers. No one had seen or heard anything.

After their investigation, the carabinieri made their reports to Comandante Greco.

The beating was blamed on the Fascio Siciliani. Greco promised the mine owners arrests from the assault would be forthcoming.

CHAPTER 51

General Morra's troops were encamped in tents just outside of Lercara Friddi, just in case the Fascio thought of destroying any other government property or were bold enough to form another boycott or demonstration.

The general, of course, was a guest of the Rose family at the mansion Villa Lisetta, even though the owners were now back in England and onto their next business venture. A full, local, servant staff was at the estate and saw to the generals every need.

Morra invited local officials for an impromptu meeting at Villa Lisetta. Comandante Greco, Mayor Sartorio, the general's Vice-Prefect Sorce, the local prosecutor, and the town's Magistrate were among the invitees.

Drinks were served, and English type hors d'oeuvres were offered. The guests sat in comfortable, club chairs with the general holding court in a high-backed, wing chair.

"Gentleman, I believe that after the rout of the Fascio here in Lercara Friddi and your diligent efforts to round-up and arrest the insurgents, we have broken the back of these confused communists. I've received a telegram from Prime Minister Crispi applauding your conscientious work on his behalf and that of the Italian government," Morra announced.

A polite applause broke out in the room.

"I am not one who makes guarantees easily, but mark my words, by the middle of January, just a few short weeks away, The Fasci Siciliani, or whatever they call themselves now, will be disbanded and the traitorous scoundrel leaders will be in prison or dead," Morra declared.

Mayor Sartorio, his administration attacked verbally in the streets by the Nicolosi family, rose from his chair to speak.

"I must say that General Morra and his officers and soldiers did everything they could to control that angry mob on Christmas day. Comandante Greco and his men are still looking for a few of the Fascio leaders who will soon be arrested and tried for treason and complicity in the deaths that occurred here. I have advised the Comandante that some members of the Nicolosi family have aided and abetted the Fascio. His investigation is underway, and there is no doubt in my mind that arrests of these predators will soon be made." Sartorio sounded like the classic politician he was.

Comandante Greco rose to speak.

"May I add an important point, please? Yesterday, a manager at the Sartorio mine was brutally beaten by three, unknown men. Our investigation into the assault is continuing, but we believe that someone within the Fascio ordered the gabbelloto to be accosted and beaten, nearly to death, I might add. The victim is in the clinic instead of the cemetery. I went to the clinic to interview him myself, and the manager has no idea who would have done this to him. He believes he has no enemies. He could barely talk, but it is his opinion the Fascio was responsible for the atrocity.

Sartorio then stated, "I have ordered the toll houses be rebuilt. There is no way that approved taxes will not be collected due to of the destruction of this government property. I have been advised the new toll houses will be erected within a week's time."

Vice Prefect Sorce was next to add to the discussion.

"I have a communication from the prosecutor in Palermo that a tribunal of Judges will be selected for a trial of the Fasci leaders. Signore Bernardino Verro has so far avoided apprehension. We are aware that Verro is seeking passage to escape to Tunis. All outbound ships are being closely monitored for both Verro and Nicola Barbato from Piana de Greci, that other notorious, Fasci leader. No doubt, due to Verro and Barbato's involvement in the Fascio in Corleone and here in Lercara Friddi, they will see significant prison time once they are arrested and tried."

General Morra followed his Vice Prefect.

"Within a few days, I will join my men to march to Marineo. Our intelligence committee has informed me that there may be trouble brewing there. We will handle Marineo just as we have other towns such as Caltauturo, Giardinello, Monreale, and here in Lercara. I am certain that very soon, whatever is left of these communists, will be quickly eliminated."

"With the General's permission, I would like to offer a toast to him and his men for pulling our town away from disaster," Mayor Sartorio declared.

Everyone rose and offered their glasses to Morra who remained seated.

"Our thanks to the General for a job well done and for God-speed in finalizing the Fasci once and for all! Salute!" Sartorio pronounced.

CHAPTER 52

Just before the new year, Salvatore Todaro had made all of his inquiries for Maria's son, Aspanu.

The lovers met in the old widow's apartment for their usual rendezvous. Todò and Maria made passionate love like never before.

After their session was over, Todò asked Maria to make some coffee. He had something important to tell her.

"Maria, are you certain you want Aspanu to leave here, to leave his family for America? I can find good work for the boy. Easy work, not like he was forced to do like a slave in danger every moment of his life," Todò stated.

"My love, of course I want my son to be near me always. But this town has no future for my boy. He has suffered so much, I truly believe that he is better off putting this life behind him with a fresh start in a country where he can make his name in any field he chooses. Please forgive me but the life you lead is not what I want for my son. Do you want what you do for *your* son?"

"No. But I want him to always be respected."

"He will always be respected because of who is father is. But if you are gone?" Maria asked.

"We watch over our own."

"But my Aspanu is not blood to you. He has a kind spirit I would not want him to lose."

"I understand your situation fully, Maria. Are you willing to never see your son again? He can go to America, make a life for himself, and never return to you. Do you realize that, Maria?" Todò asked.

"I have thought of that. If Aspanu is happy after all he has been through, I would be excited for him to make a better life," Maria replied.

"Your love for your son is so strong that you are willing to lose him?"

"He will always be in my heart and in my soul. I can never lose him," Maria stated. She smiled knowing Aspanu's happiness would be more important than the void with which she would have to live.

"I can now tell you arrangements can be made to get the approval for Aspanu to go to America and stay with your family."

"How will I afford to pay for these arrangements? How can I pay for his passage? I have nothing. I have no hope to even save enough to feed my other children and see Aspanu off to a new life. I must tell you, I will never trade my other sons as I did Aspanu for money. I would rather die."

Todò looked at his lover, convinced she clearly did not understand his intentions.

"So long as I have breath you will never want for food again. But, I have one more question. What if I arranged for your son to get legitimate work here in Lercara, work that is not in the life of men of honor?" Todò probed.

"Every day my son suffered working down in the mines I prayed for a way to end his misery. Far away America was my dream for him. His life in Lercara will always be a life of bad memories for my boy," Maria insisted.

Todò smiled at Maria with deep affection in his eyes. He replied to her with certainty.

"Everything will be taken care of. The application for his immigration will be pushed through. When he arrives in New York, friends of ours will see that he will bypass normal processing. He will be under our protection on the ship and beyond. The promise of employment that is required will be unquestioned. Even his transportation to the ship in Palermo will be of no concern for you."

"You can do all of this?"

"I have already started. The wheels are in motion. I want you to have Aspanu meet with me. I must explain to him that he is about to become a stranger in a new world. I will speak to him like he is my own son. When he understands what he is about to do, he will be with your cousins within a matter of weeks," Todò assured her.

"I have to ask you a question, my love. Something that has been on my mind. That pig of a man, Modica, the gabbelloto at the mine. I have heard that he was beaten so badly that he nearly died. Was that by your men?"

"I have no idea what you are talking about, Maria. A man like that has many enemies. What does that have to do with your son starting a new life in America?"

Maria looked at Todò to see if he was being truthful. He showed no sign of deceit.

"Why are you doing this for me?" Maria blurted.

"It's very simple, Maria. I love you. Isn't that enough?"

That same day, Aspanu was now on his fifth day of freedom from the slavery of the mine. Every time he slept, he dreamt of working side by side with Carlo. In some of his dreams, Signore Alia would be smiling at his carusi, singing his work songs.

Aspanu's longing to see Nina was overwhelming. He couldn't bear to return to the mine to catch a glimpse of Nina while she worked at the calcaroni. Aspanu waited, sitting on the ground in the cold, winter, air, on the road she always walked from the mine to her home. He saw the miners and the carusi as they trudged down that same road he himself took every day. Nina never appeared.

Aspanu ran toward the middle of town to the street where Nina lived. He walked by the Miceli house twice before he realized the home was now vacant. A pit of pain entered his stomach. *What could have happened?* he asked himself. Aspanu went to the window and peered inside. Nothing! No furniture, no beds, no candles. The house was abandoned.

Panic set in. Aspanu walked in a circle in total disbelief. The boy was beside himself. His head began to throb and his rapid breathing caused him to become light headed. After a few moments, he gathered his thoughts and calmed himself.

Aspanu walked to the next house, knocking loudly on the front door. An old woman and man came to the door. The man yelled at Aspanu for startling them. The boy took off his cap, holding it in his hands below his rope belt.

"I am sorry, signore. I am a friend of the Miceli family. I came to pay a visit, and I see the house is now empty. Can you tell me if they have moved?" Aspanu asked.

"A few days ago. The family has left Lercara," the old man stated. He started to close the door. Aspanu begged another question.

"Signore, can you please tell me where they have gone?"

The man stepped from the door and grabbed Aspanu by his arm.

"If you are a friend of the family, you should know where they went. We are not in the habit of talking about our neighbor's business. Now, get off this street unless you want me to put my foot into your ass!"

The old man waved his hand for his wife to get away from the entrance then slammed the door in Aspanu's face.

Aspanu ran to the home on the other side of the Miceli house. He was met again with a similar Sicilian response. "I know nothing!" the lady of the house responded.

Nina was gone.

CHAPTER 53

Signora Miceli, Nina's mama, had had enough of the horrible surroundings in Lercara Friddi. There seemed to be a daily tragedy about which to either see or hear. Seeing the carusi walking back from the mines in the evenings, slogging back from their servitude, both pale and exhausted, was heartbreaking to her. Townspeople were dying at a rapid pace, their coffins were carried, virtually every day, into the eight churches with many of the caskets small enough for one man to carry.

A natural death from old age was expected, although rampant diseases, starvation, and accidents were seemingly a curse on the people of Lercara.

Signora Miceli watched as her daughter started to become a beautiful, young woman. The mine was no place for a young girl to be working, nor were the sun-baked fields. Nina had told her Mama some of the things the older carusi would say to her, along with the rude and disrespectful cat calls aimed at the sweet, young lady. This was no place for Signora Miceli to raise her two daughters.

With her aging mother and aunt, Nina, and her other daughter, Signora Miceli, under cover of darkness, with the help of two, male cousins, piled the family and all their belongings into a horse-drawn, canvas-covered cart.

No one in Lercara Friddi knew Signora Miceli was relocating to the far away town of Bagheria, near Palermo. Her late husband's sister worked for a wealthy family in Bagheria where Nina would be taught to be a seamstress and Signora Miceli would find work as a domestic.

It was time to say goodbye to the family members who rested in the Lercara cemetery.

"Mama, before we leave Lercara, can I say goodbye to my friends Carlo and Aspanu?" Nina asked. It was the morning of their brave and bold move.

"NO! Are you suddenly boy crazy? Now go be useful. Help nonna and zia Rosa pack their bags. We are leaving tonight, no one in this accursed place will ever be able to follow us," Signora Miceli stated firmly.

Nina's feelings were mixed with the happiness of never returning to the sadness and stink of the mines and the pit she had in her stomach from the idea of never seeing Aspanu and Carlo again.

CHAPTER 54

New Years Day... 1894

It was New Year's Day morning and Maria Salerno brought her younger children to stay with her mother for a few hours.

Todò was coming to her home. Not for an assignation. Todò was coming to meet Aspanu.

Aspanu knew Signore Todarò was a friend of his mama and had some important things to tell them. Maria asked her son to help tidy the small house for their visitor, and he complied, by sweeping and dusting around. Maria lit all of the votive candles to help sweeten the air and cast some light into the room. She baked a loaf of bread and some biscotti to give the place a homey aroma and to serve to their guest.

Todò arrived, dressed in a dark suit, necktie, and his fedora.

"Good morning, Signore Todaro," Maria greeted her lover formally. "This is my son, Aspanu. Aspanu, please shake Signore Todaro's hand."

"My pleasure to meet you, Signore Todaro," Aspanu said. He shook the man's hand like a gentleman.

"The pleasure is all mine, I'm sure, Aspanu. Signora Salerno, may I ask your son to address me as Todò?"

"As you wish, Signore."

"So, would you please call me Todò as well?"

Maria nodded, smiling politely.

Maria put on a pot of black coffee, offering Todò a seat at the kitchen table.

"Your Mama tells me you are no longer working at the mines." Todò stated.

"Yes, Signore Todarò...I mean, Todò. I am not used to being home during the day."

"I'm certain you must be happy not to have to be underground most of the day."

"Yes, I'm very happy about that."

"And what are you planning to do for work now?"

"I'm not sure, but I think I would enjoy working in construction or laying bricks...something outdoors," Aspanu answered. The boy was a bit shy. He looked at his mama when he answered Todò.

Maria tilted her head in Todò's direction to signal her son to look at their guest.

"I have a question for you, if you don't mind?" Todò offered.

Suddenly, there was a soft knock at the door. Maria got up from her seat, leaving Todò and her son at the table.

Maria opened the door to two, burly men with wide smiles.

"Ahh, my friends are here with a gift for you, Aspanu," Todò exclaimed.

Aspanu was puzzled as one of the men carried a covered birdcage to the table.

"Go ahead, Aspanu. Remove the cover," Todò blurted.

Maria had no idea what to expect.

Aspanu removed the drape. He couldn't believe his eyes.

It was Beppe the goldfinch. The bird was jumping from one side of the cage to the other. Beppe began tweeting and pecking at the wooden bars of the cage.

"IT'S BEPPE!" Aspanu screamed.

Aspanu began to cry. Through his tears he brought his face close to the cage and began talking to the bird.

"Hello, Beppe. I thought I would never see you again. You are my pretty, little bird," Aspanu said.

The two mafiosi became choked up at the sight of the reunion. Maria cried lightly into a handkerchief.

Beppe clearly recognized the boy. The bird looked up at Aspanu, jumping to the bar, holding himself near the boy's face.

"And like you, Aspanu, your Beppe will never have to work in the mines again," Todò announced.

"Thank you, Todò. How did you know of Beppe? How did you get him? How did you ...?"

"Your mama told me about the bird. My friends here were kind enough to fetch him for you."

"Thank-you both. This is the best gift I have ever received," Aspanu said to the smiling men.

Todò nodded to his men. They left the house without saying a word.

Maria took a few almonds from her cupboard and ground them with her mortar and pestle. She handed the nuts to Aspanu. Aspanu, glowing with happiness, fed Beppe through the bars with his fingers.

"Now, when you have finished, I have a few things to say to you," Todò stated.

After a minute or two, Aspanu dropped the crushed almonds into the birds feeding cup. He walked to Todò and hugged him tightly. Maria's tears flowed again.

Aspanu returned to his seat to listen to what Todò had to say.

"How would you like to start a whole new life, Aspanu? What would you say about going to stay with your cousins in America?"

Aspanu was dumbfounded. His mind raced, but he couldn't respond.

"Mama said you would start all over, find a new profession, and have many opportunities for your life, but it is your decision to make."

Aspanu looked at his mama, still stunned by Todò's words.

"My son, you have lived in hell for four years. I am happy that you can go and start a new life. Our cousins will take you in and help you to find whatever it is that you can do to live a better life," Maria uttered.

"But Mama, when will I see you and my brothers and sister? Can you come to America, too?"

"My life is here for the moment. Perhaps we can visit one day. The important thing is that you get to make a better life. You have more than earned this chance," Maria declared. Her smile to Aspanu masked her true feelings.

"I have made the arrangements for you, Aspanu. Understand you are not forced to leave. The voyage to America is a chance of a lifetime but only if you want it. You can have the time you need to make your decision. If you decide to stay, there is no one who will disrespect your judgment," Todò stated.

"And Beppe?"

"The bird goes wherever you go. I will see to that," Todò responded.

Aspanu looked at his mama for her to help him with his decision. Maria smiled at her son, her glimmering eyes reflecting the candles.

"I am not afraid. I will go to America."

Todò told Aspanu he would send for him in a few days to explain to all the details. The man of honor drank his coffee and said his goodbyes. Maria fought the urge to jump into her lover's arms.

After Todò left, Aspanu played with Beppe for a while. Maria washed the coffee cups and was preparing to get her children from their nonna.

"Mama, I have a question. Will you marry Todò one day?"

"Aspanu! Why do you ask such a question?"

"Because I see how Todò looks at you and how you look at him. I can tell you love each other."

CHAPTER 55

The year 1894 arrived with little celebration or fanfare in Lercara Friddi.

The Christmas day massacre still weighed heavily on the minds and souls of the population along with the extreme recession which kept so many bellies empty.

Lercara Friddi's impoverished economy had devastated the morale of the vast majority of its townspeople.

Aside from the unpleasant aroma of sulfur, a constant reminder of the slave labor that plagued the town for decades, starvation and malnutrition turned the population into desperate thieves and burglars.

The town that was once called Little Palermo because of its large population and active commerce had seen so much hardship that immigration began to decimate the community. Homes were abandoned, business were closed and boarded up, garbage was piling up in the streets, and the two, leading, political factions, the Sartorio and the Nicolosi families, did nothing but point fingers at one another.

In Rome, Prime Minister Crispi and his administration declared a state of emergency to arrest every Fasci Siciliani leader, dissolve all of the organizations, and continue to use brutal force to achieve these goals. The death toll had been sounded for the workers' union and the slavery of the carusi was to continue in spite of unenforced rules and laws to not employ very young children to work in the mines.

The mine owners and land owners throughout Sicily had effectively won the right to treat the workers any way they pleased in the interest of higher profits.

Aspanu knew nothing about politics and couldn't care less. His mind was on the loss of his dear Nina to parts unknown and his friend Carlo who had been diagnosed as a paraplegic.

Aspanu tried to visit Carlo every day. Some days were better than others. Carlo was in denial of the seriousness of his injury from the soldier's bullet.

"Aspanu, did you bring me a hard candy again today, my friend and partner?" Carlo asked.

"Maybe next time, Carlo. I would have to steal one for you. There are no luxuries left…oh…wait…what do I have here in my pocket? So, I see I have a hard, lemon candy just for you," Aspanu joked. He unwrapped the sweet and placed it in Carlo's mouth.

"You trickster. You wait until I get better. I will chase you all the way to the sea," Carlo announced.

"You will need a fast donkey to catch me, Carlo, besides, I have some news to share with you."

"I hope it's good news. There is not much happening around here that is good. When that dog of a mayor used that pig of a general to attack the Fascio, all hope was lost for the workers. But don't despair, Aspanu. We will rise again, stronger than ever," Carlo spouted.

Aspanu thought to himself, "My poor friend. He thinks he will walk at the head of another rally. He will never learn that both are impossible."

"Carlo, I went past Nina's house the other day. I noticed that it was empty. I think they moved away. No one knows to where," Aspanu announced.

Carlo's smile turned to rage.

"Lies, that is impossible. Where would they move to and why? Why would she move and not tell me, not even say goodbye? You are a liar! You are just trying to keep her to yourself, you bastard. How could you do such a thing? When I'm up and walking, I will beat you like Modica beat us, you just wait."

"Carlo, they have moved, I swear on my Mama. She never said goodbye to me either. The whole family has left Lercara."

"And I suppose you will go and try to find her now," Carlo seethed.

"No, my friend. I have more news to tell you. Soon I will be going to America like so many others from Lercara. It's impossible to earn a living here, and I will not go back into those mines. My mama has made arrangements for me to begin a new life. I will be staying with cousins in New York."

Carlo's eyes darted from left to right as he could not move his neck at all.

"Go then, go now...get out of my house, you will leave me crippled and alone like this, you son of a ..."

Carlo was unexpectedly interrupted.

276

"Carlo! Stop that kind of talk to your only friend. Aspanu has done nothing wrong," Signora Panepinto said. She was out in front of the house and heard Carlo raising his voice. She rushed inside.

"Aspanu, forgive him. Your friend is having a bad day today. Come back and see him tomorrow," Carlo's Mama advised.

"Let him go to America. See if I will care!" Carlo screamed.

"Carlo, you must control yourself. Keep your mouth still," Signora Panepinto demanded.

Carlo tried to spit at Aspanu, but instead, his saliva fell onto his own face.

Aspanu, sadness etched across his face, turned on his heels and left the house.

A few days later in Palermo, the Central Committee of the Fasci Siciliani had an emergency meeting to discuss the future of the movement.

At that meeting, the founder of the Fascio in Catania, Giuseppe De Felice Giuffrida, a renowned journalist and socialist and anarchist stood up for the Fascio to take advantage of the state of emergency that was now ordered by Prime Minister Crispi. Giuffrida wanted a full-out revolution in Sicily. Some of the Fasci leadership pled for a non-violent solution for the workers' cause. Too many peasants had already paid with their lives for the union.

The majority of Fascio leaders supported a peaceful solution and issued a written appeal for the workers to remain calm and resist any emotion to provoke the government and General Morra. The majority ruled no further violence or retaliation would be acceptable.

Arrest orders were issued for Giuffrida and other founding members of the Fasci. Bernardino Verro and Nicola Barbato boarded the ship Bagnara to escape to Tunis. They were arrested and imprisoned.

Like the bullet that crippled the carusu Carlo Panepinto, the spine of the Fasci Siciliani was cut in two.

CHAPTER 56

Maria Salerno and her son, Aspanu, were waiting for word from Todò. Days flew by until it was over a week Todò had not gotten back to them. Maria had a nervous feeling that maybe her lover had second thoughts about helping her son immigrate to America, or possibly wanted to end their intimate relationship, or maybe worse. Todò was not exactly in the most secure line of work. Anything may have happened. Maria rung her hands together hour after hour.

Aspanu and his mother had a heart-to-heart talk one evening after the younger children had been tucked in their beds.

Aspanu always felt like an adult, like the man of the house when his Mama served him coffee. Especially when it was served to him in his late Papà's cup.

"Perhaps going to America is not a good idea after all," Aspanu lamented.

"Why do you say that, my son?" Maria asked. Secretly, she was beginning to wonder the same thing.

"Todò seemed like he would snap his fingers and I would be looking at that new Statue of Liberty in New York. Then Carlo made me feel badly that I would be leaving him here, all crippled up without friends. And then there is Nina," Aspanu stated.

"Nina? What are you talking about Aspanu? Who is Nina?"

"Mama, Nina Miceli, you know the family. They are good people. Her papà was also lost in the mines with papà. Nina worked at the mines, too. In the calcaroni. She became close friends with me and Carlo," Aspanu announced.

"Close friends? Holy baby Jesus! What is close friends?"

"Mama, I will marry Nina one day...I swear it!"

Maria sat down at the kitchen table to steady herself.

"Aspanu, do you have a fever? How can you talk about a girl like this? Marriage? You are still a...still very young. People don't discuss things like marriage at your age. What kind of girl is this anyway, whose mother lets her be a 'close' friend? Madonna mia, what has happened to our world?" Maria asked rhetorically. When Maria said 'close', her voice raised three octaves and her eyebrows seemed to raise to the top of her head.

"I have to find her, Mama. Nina and her family left Lercara a week ago, and no one knows where they went. I will search all of Sicily until I see her again," Aspanu raved.

"Oh, my God! My son is crazy! You are girl crazy. What do you know of girls? Her mother...only God will know what that mother will do if she lets her daughter become close to two boys. You will not go searching for this Nina or anyone else. As far as Carlo is concerned, he is crippled in bed because he became involved with dangerous things, and dangerous people. That is why I didn't want you anywhere near that square on Christmas day, yet you lied to me. But by the grace of God, you are not in your grave or lying crippled next to Carlo," Maria preached.

"But he is my friend, Mama. How can I just leave him?"

"Aspanu, mind my words now. Nonna and bisnonna, your grandmother and great grandmother always said to me, 'you are not your brother's keeper.' You are responsible to live your life the best you can. You are to forget Carlo; only God can help that poor boy. And you are to forget this little girl. There is plenty of time to meet girls in America when you are older. Santa Rosalia! Please protect this boy. Maybe the fumes from the mines have made him stupid," Maria wailed.

"Mama, what kind of man forgets his friends? I will never forget Carlo, and Nina will be my wife one day. That is all that you have to be concerned about. I will not go to America!"

Just then, a soft tapping was heard at the door to the home.

Maria put her two hands to her mouth. She was frozen in place, her eyes widened like the size of mezza tazze saucers. "It's Todò!" Maria exclaimed. Aspanu opened the front door.

At the door stood one of the men who delivered Beppe.

"Good evening, Signora. Todò asked for me to bring your son to him. Alone!"

Maria and Aspanu looked at each other with blank stares.

Todò's man walked Aspanu into the social club. It was evening, and the room was dark, illuminated by only a few candles and an old oil lamp which cast huge shadows all over the room. The feeling in the club was melodramatic with dark men, who wore full suits and hats, playing cards with few words being said.

Aspanu, suffering with a serious streak of shyness, approached the table with caution where Todò was having his coffee with anisette. The boy's lowered head, and his carusi cap in his hands, demonstrated Aspanu's uneasiness around older men. Walking into a club with men of honor as occupants, had Aspanu's knees shaking.

"Aspanu! How are you? How is your family?" Todò asked.

"All good, Signore. All good," Aspanu's voice quivered.

"So, tell me. Do you still wish to go to America? To New York?"

Aspanu did not reply with words. The young man's look and silence said enough.

"There is no obligation for this to be your destiny. But, tell me, why you have changed your mind?

Todò finished his coffee, placed the cup on the table, folded his right leg over his left, sat back in his chair...his body language telling Aspanu he was ready for a long explanation.

Aspanu hesitated. Todò stared.

"Well, first I feel badly that I am leaving my friend, Carlo, who is now crippled in his bed. We have been together as babies and worked in the mines together. To leave him now seems bad to me," Aspanu offered.

"You said first. Is there more?" Todò asked.

"Yes, Signore, there is a girl I want to marry one day. She used to live here in Lercara. She has moved away and I want to find her. Her name is Nina Miceli."

Oh, God! One pubic hair has the strength of twenty horses, Todò thought to himself.

"And? Any other reasons?"

"Well, I will miss my family, too, I suppose. That's all."

A young man brought a glass of red wine in a small glass to the Mafioso. Aspanu was served a glass of a lemon-sugar drink.

"These are the reasons of a boy. A man makes his decisions and fulfills them. You are not ready to make bold steps for your future. Best that you wait until hair grows on your balls and we can maybe consider you a man," Todò uttered. His tone was quick and sarcastic.

"Todò, I have been a man for a while now. Mama told me that I was the man of the family. I worked like an animal for my family. Here, look at my shoulders, one droops down. Look at my arms—too long for my body. I am a man!"

"No, Aspanu, you are a donkey. People point you in a direction, and you move things. A man makes decisions which will improve his position. See that boy who brought us drinks? He is still a mule. But, he is working here so one day he can sit in my chair and have a mule bring his coffee and wine. He is trying to do something. You, my dear Aspanu, you need more time at your Mama's apron. I will cancel the arrangements for now until you are ready," Todò advised.

"So, what about my reasons for wanting to stay? Are they not that of a man or loyalty…respect?"

"A friend who will lay in misery and die with or without you? A girl who can open her legs when your back is turned? Your family? Who, maybe one day, you can send for to America, and they can live a better life? Better you stay here. I can get you work as a mule somewhere."

"I am not a mule!" Aspanu seethed.

"Maybe not. Maybe half-man, half-mule."

"And this trip is all fixed for me? Like I am a big shot to get things fixed for me?"

"Aspanu, everything is fixed. Everything!   The Christmas massacre was fixed. Stop being a mule, will you please?

Aspanu paused for a moment trying to process Todò's words about the massacre in Lercara.

"Vaffanculo ...I am going to America! I will show everyone that Aspanu Salerno is a real man," Aspanu yelled.

The other mafiosi sitting in the darkened club raised their glasses to Todò.

They all knew he was giving the right advice to the former carusu.

CHAPTER 57

From the Lercara Bassa train station, smoke from the incoming locomotive could be seen in the distance. A sound of the distant whistle signaled the train would arrive in a few minutes.

Aspanu, his mother, grandmother, great aunt, and his siblings all looked down the track in anticipation of the train's arrival. None of them had ever boarded a train throughout their entire lifetimes.

Friends of Todò had arranged for the family to be taken to the station by horse-drawn wagon. Todò could not see the boy off on his journey for many obvious reasons.

What the mafioso did for Aspanu was make certain every aspect of the boy's trip was arranged and overseen up until the time he was greeted in New York harbor by his Miceli relatives. Everything was paid for. The train ride to Palermo, the passage on a steamer ship from Palermo to Naples to New York, the payoff to the passenger who would watch over the boy, and the payoff to the immigration inspector at Ellis Island.

The paperwork and the promise of employment and place of residency was all letter-perfect. Aspanu would arrive in New York with fifty dollars, American money, in his pocket when most immigrants had a fraction of that amount.

Beppe the bird had already been sent to New York to Pietro Miceli and his wife, Dorotea. Beppe traveled in the Captain's cabin of a friendly freighter with goods that were stolen by men of honor being sent to other men of honor in New York City. The bird's passage was free as a sign of respect for the friendship the now international mafia enjoyed.

Maria had packed her son's valise, which she tied with string as the latches would no longer close properly, with the few clothes her son had. Todò bought the boy a new cap. His tattered, carusi cap would be kept by his mother as a memento of the desperate times they had and the sacrifice her son had made for the family.

The old shoes he wore would be the only pair Aspanu would bring to America.

Mama also packed Aspanu's father's coffee cup, wrapping it well for the long journey. Religious cards, Santa Rosalia, Santa Barbara, and Santa Maria Constantinople would protect Aspanu on his crossing of the great Atlantic Ocean.

Finally, the friscalettu Aspanu's father played almost every night when he returned from working in the sulfur mines was wrapped in the safety of a wool blanket.

Hugs and tears became tighter and wetter as the train approached the station.

"My dear son. I cannot tell you how proud I am of your courage to make a better life for yourself. I hope one day, I will join you in America, God willing," Maria said. She did everything in her power not to sob.

Aspanu's eyes were full of tears, but he fought hard so they didn't stream down his face. His siblings were too entranced by the locomotive's size, steam, and noise as it pulled into the station.

Aspanu boarded the train with his tied valise, his new hat, and a sack with some dried fruit, cheese, bread, and salami that was to hold him over for a while. He ran to open a window of the train car. His family all waved and blew kisses, his nonna blessed herself so many times it seemed as though she had an affliction.

Aspanu gazed at his family until they were just a dot in the distance. He was off to his new life in America.

The countryside flew by as Aspanu tried to take in every hill and mountain, every town and valley, every farm and glen. He never expected to see such beautiful countryside while working in the dregs of the earth for almost half of his young life.

Aspanu would stare at a hilltop town, and close his eyes, as if he were taking a photograph with his memory.

He wanted so much to take the friscalettu from his bag, but his Mama had warned him to wait at least until he was on the ship, where he would have plenty of time to play the flute. His voyage would take a full sixteen days to arrive at Ellis Island.

When the train pulled into the magnificent, seven-year-old Palermo Centrale railway station, Aspanu got those butterflies in his stomach, similar to what he had on the first day of work in the Gardner-Rose sulfur mine. Similar, but not identical. The tingling Aspanu had this day was one of excitement and anticipation, rather than simply fear.

Aspanu could never have imagined the enormity of the station. The size of the trains, the height of the ceiling once inside, the yelling from the conductors, the sounds of steam letting loose from locomotives, and the shrill whistles, added by the throngs of people who all seemed to be running somewhere, stopped the boy in his tracks.

"Excuse me, are you Gaspare Salerno from Lercara Friddi?" A man in a long coat, stovepipe hat, wearing a gray and brown handlebar moustache asked Aspanu.

"Yes, I am Gaspare Salerno."

"I am Silvio. Your friends at home have asked me to get you to the ship. We have some time before you have to board. Are you hungry, young man?"

"A bit, yes."

"Come, I know a nice spot for fish near the pier. We will enjoy a lunch and chat a bit before you board. May I call you Aspanu?"

"Of course, Signore Silvio, everyone calls me Aspanu."

Silvio navigated Aspanu through the bustling crowd, making sure the local pickpockets and panhandlers stayed clear of the boy. All Silvio had to do was sneer at someone to turn their spines into ricotta. He was an escort at the moment, but Silvio would be called upon to do whatever he was asked to do by the men of honor for whom he worked. Silvio could strangle someone before lunch, then sit down for a beautiful repast of spaghetti and meatballs, in their honor.

As they approached the piers, Silvio stopped and raised his bulky arm.

"Look, Aspanu, that is the boat that will take you to America. The Letimbro. You will never forget that name and this special day. It may seem sad at first to leave Sicily, but in America, the streets are paved with gold. If you are smart, you will do well there. If not, then you will come back here and wish you were smarter," Silvio preached.

Silvio pointed his other arm.

"Allura, so there is the restaurant. I'm starved!" Silvio bellowed.

The word restaurant may have been a stretch by Silvio. No sign on the outside of the one-story, tar paper building. There was no menu, no waiters, with working class men, mostly ruddy stevedores and weary sailors, some just drinking wine or some Irish Whiskey. Long, wooden tables and rickety chairs stood beneath the plaster walls, with an oil-stained photograph of Victor Emmanuel I peering down on the patrons.

Behind an unpainted, wood counter, a very overweight woman wearing an off-white, sauce-stained dress and a black, wrap-around head cover, handed dishes of steaming spaghetti with various types of fish to the seedy and grumpy-looking diners.

In the tiny kitchen, screaming at everyone from the fat women to the boys who worked shucking clams and cleaning fish, was the proprietor of the "establishment." Filthy in appearance and language, Salvo De Matteo had spent most of his life in prison for a variety of anti-social behaviors up to and including manslaughter. The eatery was left to him by his father as more of an insult than an asset.

"Wayyyy! Don Silvio, now my day is complete!" The heavy woman exclaimed.

"Good day, Josie, I have a young guest so I don't want to hear any foul language from you today," Silvio blurted.

From behind the counter came Salvo. He wiped his hands on his apron which may have been white at one time.

"Don Silvio, I kiss your hand," Salvo said, his scraggly beard brushed against Silvio's hand.

"Bring us some food. There is a ship leaving in an hour. And some coffee for me, and a lemon drink for my friend here," Silvio ordered.

Everyone in the place knew of Silvio. Heads lowered into their food or drink so as not to make eye contact. Respect was the feeling in the room. Or maybe it was fear?

Aspanu ate some delicious clams and shrimp in a red sauce with fettuccine and some crusty, fresh bread. Silvio devoured a dish of pasta con sarde, with toasted bread crumbs and three cups of mezza tazze coffee.

Silvio didn't say much while he ate. He constantly looked around the room and at the door as if he was expecting someone.

Aspanu's mind began to wonder. "Could it be true I will never see Nina again? Why am I leaving? I know we are destined to be together and have a family. How can I leave her here in Sicily?"

A very short man appeared at the door, scanning the clientele of Salvo's joint. His eyes met with Silvio's, and he waddled over to the man of honor's table.

The little man removed his hat as he approached Silvio. He whispered in the mafioso's ear and handed him an envelope. Silvio put the envelope into his inside vest pocket as the man walked off.

"Let's go, Aspanu. It's time for you to take your journey," Silvio announced.

CHAPTER 58

Aspanu gazed up at the SS Letimbro, shading his eyes from the sun. He had never seen a boat, never mind a passenger cargo ship.

The ship had one funnel and two masts, and at almost three hundred feet in length the Letimbro's iron shell made Aspanu scratch his head in wonder.

As passengers got in line to show their documents, Silvio waved to an officer of Navigazione Generale Italiana, the ship owners.

The men of honor had friends in all the right places. There would be no waiting for Aspanu. Silvio walked the boy to the front of the line.

"Aspanu, have a great voyage and a wonderful new life. Come back to visit us. Sicily will always be in your blood," Silvio stated.

"Thank-you, Signore Silvio. I will do my best."

Silvio reached into his jacket and pulled out the envelope the short man had given him earlier.

"Here is a little token for you. Out of our respect to Todò. Put this into your shoe. You will be safe during this voyage. A good friend of mine will watch for you. If anyone bothers you on this ship it will be their last voyage and a wet grave for them," Silvio warned.

Aspanu was momentarily shocked by Silvio's words. The boy looked down the ship's bow as the engines were being tested. Black smoke billowed from the funnel.

Two, junior officials were seated at a small desk in front of the walkway up to the ship. The officer who knew Silvio, whispered into the ear of one of his subordinates, who took a too-quick look at Aspanu's paperwork, stamped them, and added the boy's name, age, town, and some other information to the ship's manifest.

Aspanu walked up the ramp, not believing questions were never asked of him.

The ship's speed was a maximum of eleven knots, a full sixteen days, if the weather was favorable, would be needed to reach New York Harbor. The Letimbro offered twenty, first class accommodations and room for seven-hundred, third class passengers. Aspanu would be in third class, with the rest of the 'huddled masses yearning to breathe free,' as Emma Lazarus wrote in her sonnet *The New Colossus* eleven years earlier.

Aspanu was not at all happy with his decision to leave for America. Not out of fear of a new life, language, and culture. Not because he was leaving his Mama and the rest of the Salerno clan. Carlo didn't fit into his concerns any more. Carlo was warned not to get involved with the Fasci, he gambled and he lost his future to the union. Aspanu's thoughts were of Nina. How could she marry anyone else? What would his life be without her? He would always want her as his wife...no matter who else he might be with.

Aspanu began pacing the length of the third-class steerage. His head was down, deep in thought. How could he get back to Lercara? How could he face his family? What would he say to Todò? Too many complications for a boy who suffered miserably in the bowels of the sulfur mines for so long.

"I can't go! I must be a man and find Nina. I would rather go back into the mines and work there for thirty years than lose Nina," Aspanu thought to himself. He began to mumble to himself. Some of

293

the passengers gave the boy a wide berth, thinking he might be touched in the head.

Suddenly, the loud warning whistle of the Letimbro sounded the first of three departure notices.

The sailors got into their positions to throw the ropes from their moorings. Officers began barking out orders. The ship had three hundred and seventy-two passengers on this voyage, well below the maximum.

"Now I will leave," Aspanu said aloud. He started walking toward the opening to the manway, when he remembered the envelope Silvio had given him. Aspanu opened the envelope as he walked. There were many five dollar American bills stacked inside. He couldn't count how many but decided to return the gift somehow.

As he approached the opening, suddenly he heard his name called out loudly.

"ASPANU! ASPANU!"

The boy turned to see who would know his name. His hand on the rail, Aspanu scanned the crowd for a familiar face.

"ASPANU SALERNO!" the voice shouted.

Among the hundreds in steerage he could see someone waving a kerchief.

It was Nina Miceli.

Aspanu's heart soared. "Could this be real?" he stated aloud.

Nina ran toward Aspanu, her hands up in the air.

"Aspanu, what are you doing here?"

Aspanu didn't hear her question.

"What are you doing here, Nina?"

"Mama had a plan all along. We went to Bagheria to wait for approval to leave Sicily. I was to be a seamstress, but it never happened. Our immigration papers came to us just the other day. We are going to Brooklyn to stay for a while with relatives. Me and Mama will be working in a factory or maybe will have a job as a seamstress, I really am not sure anymore. We are going to America."

Aspanu couldn't believe his ears nor his eyes. He was dumbstruck for a few moments. Nina looked at him strangely and he finally spoke.

"I, too, am going to America to stay with my Mama's cousin. Also to Brooklyn," Aspanu shouted over the second warning whistle. Sailors began shoving off the ship.

Aspanu never saw such a big smile as the one Nina gave him at that moment.

Nina grabbed Aspanu by his hand.

"Come with me. You will stay with Mama and the rest of my family for the journey," Nina commanded.

The SS Letimbro began to move, the final whistle blowing louder and longer than the first two.

Aspanu stood firm in his place. Nina was tugging at his arm.

"Nina, I was leaving the ship just now," Aspanu uttered.

"Leaving the ship? But why?"

Aspanu paused, tears ran down his cheeks. Then a big smile erupted on his face.

"To find you, Nina…to find you!"

CHAPTER 59

CHRISTMAS 1975

Nina was now ninety-eight years old. She still kept house and cooked every day. All of the children and grandchildren, and now a couple of great-grandchildren came to Nina and Aspanu's home every Sunday for dinner.

Nina never worked outside of the home. The Salernos were old school in many ways so the income was always Aspanu's responsibility. Anything inside the house was Nina's duty. As a matter of fact, they were so old-fashioned Nina never even learned to drive a car. They never ate in a restaurant. Their backyard garden helped them feed themselves and their family.

In the Morris Park section of the Bronx, everything that was needed for the family was found within a five or six-block radius of the home they built together, a two-story brick home on Randall Avenue.

All of the cousins who immigrated from Lercara Friddi and their compare, their friends, helped Aspanu build the home. Mr. and Mrs. Gaspare Salerno, Aspanu and Nina, would live upstairs and rent the bottom of the house to tenants for income.

Aspanu worked twelve hours a day, every day except Sundays, from the time he got off the boat at Ellis Island until he was eighty years old.

First, with his Mama's cousin Pietro Miceli, Aspanu was a laborer, digging ditches, laying concrete, building brick or stone walls, and any other manual labor, until he married Nina when he turned eighteen. Aspanu never went to school in America, but he learned to speak English and read and write on his own.

Another Miceli cousin, Giuseppe Miceli, helped Aspanu get a steady, city job with the New York City Transit Authority when Aspanu turned thirty.

Starting as a train cleaner, Aspanu worked his way up to mechanic, fixing trains, and then later, he worked on the city's buses. Aspanu would never miss a day's work.

Aspanu enjoyed the buses because he was no longer working underground. The years in the subway system somehow reminded him of working in the mines, but it was steady work at good pay.

Just before their three children, two boys and a girl, were to arrive for Christmas day dinner, Aspanu went into the kitchen and took Nina by the hand, leading her into their small dining room.

The dining room table was set for dinner, fifteen chairs and two baby high-chairs, were crowded around a cherry wood table that Aspanu built with his own hands in 1945.

A small breakfront with photographs of their children and grandchildren was on one wall. A carved, cherry wood buffet table, also crafted by Aspanu sat on the opposite side.

On the buffet stood plaster statues of Santa Barbara, Padre Pio, and Saint Anthony of Padua. The statuary was all adorned with rosary beads surrounded by full poinsettia plants and the funeral cards of deceased relatives and friends. A glass container next to the statues contained a chunk of yellow sulfur ore Aspanu brought back from the mines of Lercara Friddi. He looked at the ore often, always reminding him where he came from and how he had suffered.

"Aspanu, I have no time to talk now. Everyone will be here soon," Nina protested.

"Make the time for me, please, Nina. I have some things I want to say to you," Aspanu pleaded.

Nina made a crooked face but sat next to her husband of seventy-three years.

"From the very first time I saw you at the calcaroni, I knew I would marry you. That moment gave me hope and dreams when life was full of despair. I want to thank you for being my wife and giving me such a wonderful family," Aspanu said.

"So, you wait until my lasagna is burning in the oven to tell me this?"

"I'm sure it will not burn, my dear wife. Do you remember Carlo had eyes for you, too?"

"Poor Carlo! Have you lost your mind, Aspanu? We were babies then."

"I thought I would lose my mind when your Mama took you from Lercara. I swear that I would have searched all of Sicily to find you," Aspanu recalled.

"I remember like it was yesterday when I saw you on the ship. Were you really going to get off and go back home?"

"I've told you that a thousand times. It was San Antonio who found you for me."

"San Antonio finds lost keys and things like that. He doesn't find *people,* Aspanu!" Nina blurted.

'For me, he put you on that ship."

"I thought my Mama was going to throw you overboard into the water when we arrived near New York and you told her you would marry me one day," Nina remembered.

"Of course! She called me 'testa di scieccu,' head of a donkey and smashed me with her purse.

The two nonagenarians laughed out loud.

"And you never gave up asking until finally she said yes," Nina offered. Her eyes moist with happy tears.

"We did pretty good, Nina. We had a good, full life and I am grateful for every moment."

"Aspanu, are you not feeling very well? This sounds like the words of someone who is saying goodbye," Nina lamented.

Aspanu embraced Nina, kissing her softly on her lips.

"For us there will never be a goodbye. I will tell Jesus I refuse to be without you in heaven."

EPILOGUE

At the continued orders of Prime Minister Crispi, General Morra and his militia continued their butchering of the peasants who demonstrated against heavy taxes and working conditions. The General was bound and determined to obliterate any sign of the Fasci Siciliani.

The militia began using machine guns to mow down the peasants.

Eighteen workers were killed in the town of Marineo with dozens more wounded. In Santa Caterina, thirteen were shot dead for protesting, again many were wounded. Field guards, a group of vicious, cold-hearted men, hired by the land owners, used their rifles to assist the General and his men, catching the stick and stone carrying peasants in a crossfire.

In early March of 1894, the leader of the field guards, a known mafia boss, Girolamo Miceli, was acquitted in a farcical, two-day trial by a military court due to lack of evidence for his role in the killings of the workers.

In April and May of 1894, the trials of the central committee of the Fasci Siciliani were packed daily with onlookers. The leaders were kept in a joint cell inside of the Palermo courtroom. Newspapers reported the daily remarks made by the prosecutors, the persuasive defense of the Fasci members, and their attorneys, as well as remarks of the politicians, including Prime Minister Crispi who condemned the union, blaming its leaders for the death of so many peasants.

On May 30, Fasci leaders Giuseppe de Felice Giuffrida and Rosario Bosco received eighteen years in prison. Nicolo Barbato and Bernardino Verro were sentenced to twelve years each. The Fasci Siciliani was finished.

The Spanish Influenza Pandemic in 1918 was the worst natural disaster in the history of the world. An estimated five hundred million people were infected by this disease, almost a third of the earth's population. Fifty million were killed worldwide.

Aspanu never did see his family again. Twenty-five years after he left Lercara Friddi, Aspanu's mother, and all of his siblings, along with three of their infant children, died from 'La Grippe'.

On a busy street in Palermo, ten years before the pandemic, Todò was shot dead by a rival mafia faction. Maria was broken-hearted from that day until the day she died.

Doctor Alfonso Giordano, aside from his medical practice, became the mayor of Lercara Friddi for two terms. He died in July, 1915 at the age of seventy-two. He successfully treated Aspanu of anemia, caused by the hookworm before the boy immigrated to America.

Carlo succumbed to pneumonia a month after Aspanu left Sicily.

Another son of Elvira Panepinto would work as a carusu. He succumbed to a lung infection before his twentieth birthday. Elvira died in a mental hospital in Palermo at the age of eighty-two.

Monsignor Giacomo Paci served in Lercara Friddi until just before his death in 1904. He died at the ripe, old age of eighty-one.

He never disobeyed his superiors and never stood for the human rights of his parishioners.

Giuseppe Esposito turned himself in to friendly authorities in the town of his birth, Alia. While being transferred to a jail in Palermo, he escaped with the aid of the mafia. Esposito fled to New York City after a short stay in Marseilles, France.

With a new name, Vincenzo Rebello, Esposito started a new life in New Orleans where he eventually ran the illegal activities on the docks and in the produce markets. He was later deported to Italy and given a life sentence.

The FBI stated Esposito was the first mafia member to immigrate to the United States. The truth was, Esposito, or his new name Rebello, was never a true man or honor. He was simply a blood thirsty criminal.

Antonio Lucania, a sulfur miner in Lercara Friddi, and his wife Rosalia Capporelli, had several children together. One of their sons, Salvatore, born in Lercara on November 24, 1897, would immigrate at the age of nine to New York City. Salvatore would not follow his father into the bowels of the earth to mine sulfur ore. Instead, he would grow to be arguably the most powerful mafia boss in United States history. Lucania was the architect of the establishment of the mafia commission and a national crime syndicate.

In the United States, Salvatore Lucania was better known as Lucky Luciano.

A year and a half before the Christmas day massacre, Saverio Antonino Martino Sinatra was born in Lercara Friddi. His father Francesco, a shoemaker, lived at Via Regina Elena. On December 21, 1903, Sinatra immigrated to Hoboken, New Jersey. Saverio met and married Natalina Maria Vittoria Garaventa, who was born in Lumarzo,

Genoa in 1896. Saverio was younger than Natalina, and of course, he was Sicilian. Two reasons why the bride's family did not approve of a marriage.

Marty and Dolly, their Americanized names, had a son who would also never work in the mines as some of his forefathers did. Francis Albert Sinatra became a pretty well-known, saloon singer.

CPSIA information can be obtained
at www.ICGtesting.com
Printed in the USA
FFHW021902120119
50103727-54966FF